T0339849

WORLD GOVERNMENT: UTOPIAN DREAM OR CURRENT REALITY?

World Government: Utopian Dream or Current Reality?

Raymond Converse

Algora Publishing
New York

Library of Congress Cataloging-in-Publication Data —

Converse, Raymond W.
  World government: utopian dream or current reality? / Raymond Converse.
      p. cm.
  Includes bibliographical references and index.
  ISBN 978-0-87586-762-5 (trade paper: alk. paper) — ISBN 978-0-87586-763-2 (case
laminate: alk. paper) 1. International organization. 2. International cooperation. I. Title.
  JZ1318.C65775 2010
  341.2—dc22
                              2009051525

Front cover design by Algora Publishing

Printed in the United States

TABLE OF CONTENTS

Chapter 1. Is a General Peace and World Government Feasible?

Reading a small book entitled *Report from Iron Mountain on the Possibility and Desirability of Peace* (Dial Press, Inc., 1967) stimulated my thoughts about world peace forty years after that book was published. Whether the Report from Iron Mountain (hereafter simply called the report) was an officially-sanctioned report or merely the conjecture of its author does not matter in our case. The questions it brought forward are interesting in and of themselves. Could we have a world government, and if so, would we want it? In the best case unified administration can bring many benefits to a large and diverse population not least of which is peace. The Report from Iron Mountain introduces the types of problems that would arise upon any decision to attempt to establish an effective world government.

As the report indicates the establishment of an effective world government would entail the concurrent establishment of world peace. The report even concludes that the establishment of world peace may be a pre-condition to the possibility of world government. The need to satisfy this pre-condition was allegedly the reason for the report being produced.

The report defines two steps that would have to be taken before world peace could be established. The first, and probably the most important, is a detailed study to determine whether world peace is possible and if it is possible whether or not it is desirable. Second, if the determination is made that peace is both possible and desirable a process must be devised to allow for the institutionalization of a general peace. This is to say that a competent structure must be put in place to support a general peace and to detail the timing of its implementation on a worldwide scale.

To determine whether world peace is both possible and desirable we would have to conduct a detailed analysis of the current structure of society in the areas of economics, politics, sociology, and the cultural and scientific arenas. In addition, a constitutional base would have to be created that would put in place the executive, legislative, and judicial institutions necessary to establishing a general peace. The likely effects of a general peace must be analyzed as to its effects on national and world economies, on the operation of existing political tenets, on the underlying social cohesions now in operation, and lastly, its effects on existing cultural and scientific traditions. This analysis will indicate whether or not the general peace is desirable regardless of whether or not it is possible. It may be that the effects of a general peace will be so costly that the gains will not justify its institution.

Second, we would have to outline the specific actions that would be necessary to accomplish a general peace. Under this heading it might be necessary to draft a proposed constitution setting forth the necessary alterations of existing executive, legislative, and judicial institutions. This would include a detailing of the changes that would need to be made at the national and local levels of government as well as in establishing a general world government. This would include specific methods or procedures needed to ratify and institute a general peace, i.e., elections, physical buildings, and other infrastructure needed to put a general peace into operation. Lastly, specific procedures or processes would need to be detailed to counteract destabilizations that might occur in the existing economies, nation states, and social and cultural institutions.

The report begins by acknowledging that nothing approaching the scope or complexity of a general peace has yet faced mankind. There has never been a period of peace involving all of mankind. The famous Pax Romana and the peace that followed the establishment of the ancient Han Dynasty in China represent the closest example of a general peace and they were in fact far from peaceful in the sense used in the report. The report defines a general peace as the absence of both war and weapons of war. The report did not intend to include all forms of conflict or to suggest that a general peace would be the same as a problem-free existence for mankind or even any portion of mankind. It should also be kept in mind that the report was essentially aimed at determining the possibility and desirability of a general peace in relation to the United States rather than in a worldwide context.

The report next defines what it calls the "war system" that has dominated men's relations to one another since the dawn of history; and it takes the position that the establishment of a general peace would require that system to be dismantled. The system includes not only weapons and shooting wars but the "non-military functions" of the system. One of the report's tenets is that the decision to destroy all weapons of war and to forgo further shooting wars would be the easiest of the requirements to satisfy in the establishment of a general peace. It is the non-military functions of the system that the report suggests are critical in determining the possibility and desirability of peace and therefore it is this aspect of the problem upon which the report focuses.

The non-military functions of the war system are broken into several categories as follows: economic, political, social, ecological, and cultural–scientific. Each category of non-military function is then analyzed to determine exactly what would need to be altered to accomplish a general peace. After searching for a workable alternative to the war system in each category these alternatives are assessed to determine their practicality. Lastly, a conclusion is drawn in relation to the specific place occupied by the United States and its interest in a general peace.

First we will follow what the report indicates were the non-military functions of the war system in 1967. We will then attempt to determine whether or not they are the same in 2009. The economic function of the war system was seen in 1967 to be a dependable institution for the stabilization and control of national economies. This function was realized through the war systems "waste" of the products of over production. It was capable of acting as a stabilizer and control over the economy through the government's arbitrary power to manipulate this waste of assets. The national government could stimulate the economy by increasing the amount of waste within the system and it could apply a brake to the economy by reducing the amount of waste within the system. Second, the political functions of the war system were seen as the production of the permanent possibility of war. It is the permanence of possible war that provides the nation with the citizen's general acceptance of political authority. In short, the permanent threat of war requires the institution of government to secure the public from external aggression by others. As a result society generally has been able to maintain certain class distinctions to insure the obedience of the general population according to the report. Indeed, the report contends that no modern political ruling class has been successful in controlling its citizens after failing to sustain the credibility of a possible shooting war. The political functions of the war system reside in the residual war powers inherent in the nation-state system or the concept of nationalism. Third, in the area of sociology the report determined the non-military function of the war system to be the control of social dissidence and anti-social behavior generally. This function was accomplished through the manipulation of the war system such as adjusting the selective service program to draw mainly from those parts of society that produced anti-social behavior. By absorbing those in society that suffered from the effects of poverty, under education, lack of specialized training, or who suffered from minor physical or mental disabilities the system acted as a social filter. As the only credible threat to life that is also directly under the control of the government (executive branch) it is seen as the key motivational force governing human behavior. The system was capable of transforming this behavior into a binding social allegiance (patriotism). Fourth, the function of the war system in the field of ecology is seen as the only non-evolutionary device unique to humans for effective population control. The war system when properly manipulated could maintain a balance between the human population and the supplies available for human survival. Fifth, in the cultural–scientific arena the war system is seen as the traditional foundation of the value systems which have historically driven both the fine arts and science. The system has produced the subject matter and basic standard of value (war, heroes, death and life) in the creative arts. It was also the main factor motivating the forward movement of science especially technology within any given society.

The report having concluded the rendition of the non-military functions of the war system it then moved on to set forth the criteria under which any alternative offered to the war system must operate. The alternative offered is then judged by the criteria established allowing a determination of that alternatives practicality. This determination being one of the two criteria that the report had set out to be met, that is, the possibility of a general peace. The criteria established within the report are as follows. One, the report flatly concludes that no alternative to the non-military functions of the war system has yet been tested in a complex modern society and shown itself to be even remotely comparable in scale and effectiveness. This statement will be seen as true of all the non-military functions of the war system and not just those involved with economics. Granting therefore that the alternatives to be offered have yet to be tested in a modern society they are offered as the choices gathered by the report to be tested. In the economic field any alternative would have to prove itself capable of "wasting" lives and material at a rate comparable to that of the war system. In addition, any alternative system of waste would also have to show itself capable of being within the arbitrary control of the government. Two, within the political arena any alternative would be required to pose a permanent external threat comparable to that offered by a credible permanent threat of a shooting war. This threat would need to be as credible and as easy to understand by the normal citizen as is the threat of a shooting war. The alternative threat would also have to be of such a magnitude that it would require social organization (government) to oversee its control. It would also have to be of such a nature as to direct the behavior of the citizens to obedience to the commands of the state. Three, in the absence of the war system any alternative system offered in the sociological arena would be required to focus on social dissidence and anti-social behavior. In short, whatever alternative is offered it would have to be capable of absorbing and transforming any type of social dissidence, such as racial inequality, that might exist and be capable of transforming the ill will generated by this disruption into voluntary obedience to authority. The report claims that these types of behavior are most prevalent in the parts of society subject to poverty, under education, lack of technical training, etc. This being true the alternative offered would need to address how these factors could be eliminated, or at the very least, neutralized in relation to the behavior patterns incorporated in them. Four, concerning the ecological functions of the war system any alternative would need to address the problem of over population. It is suggested by the report that the war system represents the most efficient manner in which humans can be systematically destroyed (by conscious design) to assure that the number of people in existence at any one time does not exceed the materials necessary to support them. Therefore, any offered alternative will have to prove itself capable of making a decision that too many humans are now in existence and provide an efficient means of reducing that number. The report, however, adds a factor to this alternative that was not expressed as being a part of the war system, that is, the ability at the same time to provide for the controlled improvement of the human species through genetic engineering. There is no claim in the report that the war system has, or does, perform such a function, but that any alternative offered to replace the war system should also be capable of this function. Five, in the area of cultural–scientific endeavor the report suggests that the war system, although it does provide a value-system for cultural endeavors, and a motivational system for scientific progress, it is not essential to the war system. The report claims, for example, that art seems to be perfectly capable of operating outside of any type of value system. In short, the report does not conclude that an alternative system is needed in this area.

Having set forth the criteria by which to judge the alternatives to the war system the report attempts to set forth those alternatives. The reader is left to his own devices in determining the source of the alternatives offered and whether they are thought to represent the only choices or are merely an arbitrary selection by the authors. Be that as it may, the alternatives offered are sufficient to guide a detailed exploration of what might be faced by an effective world government under conditions of a general peace.

One, in the economic area the report offers three alternative solutions to the non-military functions of the war system. First, it has been proposed that a comprehensive social welfare system directed towards the maximum improvement of the general conditions of human life be instituted. Under this alternative the monies and materials expended on the existing war system would be diverted to social projects under the arbitrary control of the general government. Initially these monies would be spent upon the construction of the infrastructure needed to carry out the social goals, that is, schools, hospitals, roads, bridges, canals, railroads, sewage systems, and water treatment facilities among others. They would also include massive extensions in the existing programs of old age benefits, health insurance, disability and unemployment compensation, and other entitlement programs. In judging this alternative by the criteria set forth above the report concludes that it does not fulfill the demand that it be arbitrary in the sense of government control. In this case, at least after the initial expenditures on infrastructure are complete, the continued payments under the welfare system would become merely a part of the normal system of supply and demand, that is, they would no longer be capable of arbitrary governmental control. For this reason the alternative of a comprehensive welfare system cannot replace the war systems function as a stabilizer and controlling factor in economic fluctuations. The report does, however, accept the short term benefits that could be used in the period of capital outlay as a transition from the war system to a more comprehensive alternative. Second, it has been proposed that the military budget be converted into a gigantic space research program that incorporates unattainable goals. This system has the ability to meet the objection to the welfare alternative, that is, that it lacks the element of arbitrariness. Under the present alternative the capital expenditures would never end as the projects could be extended indefinitely. There would not be a period in which this alternative would reach a stage of pure maintenance of existing payment. For example, the first project could be the full colonization of the moon. When and if the first project has been completed it can be adjusted to accomplish the full colonization of the planet Mars and so forth. This alternative also can claim the benefit of being capable of capturing the approval of the public at large. This alternative appears to satisfy all of the judging criteria set forth by the report. It is subject to arbitrary control and can be manipulated by government authorities to either stimulate or put a brake on economic activity. It would also be in a position to "waste" both vast amounts of material goods and human lives at a terrific rate. This alternative, according to the report, also has the added benefit of being capable of being dovetailed into the solutions of the other non-military functions of the war system. Third, it has been proposed that the war system be converted into a huge ritualized inspection system. The report considers the initial portion of this alternative to be established in relation with the real need for inspection systems to insure disarmament. This initial need would include an inspection system for the verified and safe disposal of the toxic waste involved in any complete disarmament program. Once the initial real needs are satisfied the alternative would become purely a ritual performance of these inspection duties. This latter function carries with it the chance that it will not continue to win the approval of the public at large and also the chance that it will not be capable of producing the needed quantity of "waste". In short, the alternatives involved in the welfare and inspection systems fail to satisfy the criteria set forth by the report and it is concluded that only the space research alternative meets the standards required. Therefore, this alternative is accepted as the most likely candidate to replace the war system in the economic arena.

Two, in the political field the report sets forth four alternative systems to the non-military functions of the war system. It is important to remember in this area that the non-military functions of the war system acted as a guarantee that the public at large would accept the authority of government in general, and that this acceptance would be converted into a patriotic obedience to the specific government under which they lived. It is likely that the war system has been a major factor in the development of the current system of nationalism. The need to define one in relation to others has proceeded largely by the public's recognition of similarities in language, religion, customs, etc. and the need to protect them against aggression by others of a different language, religion, customary style, etc. The concept of patriotism is to a large degree based upon the public's perception that the government is providing them with protection. It is an unspoken maxim of political ideology that the major duty of any form of government is to provide its citizens with individual security especially in relation to external invasion. Therefore, any alternative to the war system will need to show that it can effectively garner the support of the public and produce something akin to patriotism. The four alternatives considered by the report in the political area are as follows. First, the report suggests that the war system be replaced with an international police force with extensive powers. This system, according to the report, would be similar to the inspection system mentioned as an alternative in economics. It is, according to the report, not compatible in the long run with the basic premise of a general peace. It subsumes the continuation of weapons of war, at least in the hands of the policing organization, and the power to use them. It is also not likely that the long continuation of an all inclusive police force would meet with public approval after the completion of whatever initial justification existed. Second, it was suggested that an understandable threat of invasion from outer space could be created. Regardless of what may have been the level of concern with invasion from outer space in 1967 it can be safely assumed that in 2009 such a threat would not be credible to the public. The sole exception to this scenario would be the threat of a collision between the Earth and an asteroid or other space object. This event, however, is to a large extent considered in the same light as obtaining a winning lottery ticket. It is possible, because it has happened in the past, but unlikely to happen in the immediate present. This alternative fails to satisfy the demand that it generate a necessary acceptance by the public for government, regardless of form, and in generating any patriotic type attachment to a specific government. Third, it has been suggested that the war system be replaced with a credible threat of an environmental nature. This would have the benefit of avoiding the problem of credibility found in the space threat alternative. In 1967 this type of threat was just beginning to come into the consciousness of the public at large. At that time it might have been necessary to "create" the seriousness of this threat to convince people of its ability to destroy them personally. In 2009, however, environmental threats have become a recognized source of personal threat comparable to the fear of external invasion in past times. For example large degrees of the public at large at least in the well educated nations of the industrial complex have accepted the fact that climate change is the result of unregulated use of fossil fuels. This same public has accepted the danger of environmental pollution in terms of future water supplies, the quality of future air supplies, and the diminution of natural resources. It is likely that a general acceptance could be generated for any reasonable proposal that would reverse these processes. It is also likely that the public would accept the shift from nationalism to world government if it could be shown that such a shift was necessary to accomplish their goals. Whether or not this type of alternative would be sufficient to generate an ongoing public perception of the need for government, and the patriotic type of allegiance to a specific world government is questionable, especially if the threat represented by environmental pollution is resolved. Regardless, however, environmental pollution is one issue that will have to be faced immediately by either the existing nationalistic system or by any world government created to replace it. Fourth, it has been suggested that a fictional alternative enemy be created. This, of course, automatically calls for the retention of the continued readiness for war. This alternative was dismissed without discussion by the report in 1967 except for the use that could be made of this concept by individual nations, such as the United States. Indeed, in 2009 just such a use may have been initiated by the US government in response to the attack it suffered on Sept. 11, 2001. This act was in essence an intentional act of insurrection intended to awaken the American public to the interest of fundamentalist Muslims in the Middle East. The US government, however, generalized the attack by calling it a "war on terrorism". In effect this created a fictional enemy capable of producing the type of fear in the public that was generated by its fear of invasion by the former Soviet Union. The threat was to some degree credible based on the success of the first attack, but has proven incapable of sustaining the level of concern necessary to allow this alternative to replace the war system. This alternative, therefore, does not satisfy the criteria set forth by the report. The final conclusion of the report in relation to politics is that no alternative yet exists which can successfully replace the non-military functions of the war system. As a result a general peace would not be desirable in relation to its inability to generate public acceptance of authority and translating that acceptance into patriotism.

Three, in the area of sociology the war system's non-military functions are seen to be two fold. First, in relation to the control function, i.e., the absorption of anti-social elements, and second, the creation of a motivation for subordinating individual needs to the needs of the government. In this area the report suggests that there are two alternatives. First, the report indicates that a large scale program similar to the Peace Corps initiated under John F. Kennedy be created. This system could and probably would operate in the same manner as the military in 1967. A social draft would be instituted targeting the same populations that were targeted under the selective service as it existed in 1967. It could however also operate, although maybe not as effectively in relation to the targeted populations, under the voluntary military system in force in the United States in 2009. This program would be specifically intended to relieve those suffering from poverty, lack of education in general, and lack of specific technical training. It would, or could, operate as a type of educational scholarship program coupled to a specific work program. It could also be used to supply useful occupations and activities to those who suffered from both physical and mental handicaps that make it difficult for them to enter into the general society. The report, although recognizing the role that could be played by such an alternative, concluded that it would be incapable of generating the level of activity needed to replace the functions of the war system. Second, it was suggested that some type of altruistic slave system could be created to replace the war system. This alternative seems to be incredulous at first glance but two points must be made concerning it. The first point is that a military based upon involuntary service, or even voluntary service generated by inability to comfortably fit into the general society, is a form of slavery itself. It must also be pointed out that throughout history one of the most effective ways of suppressing and controlling anti-social behavior was slavery. It is likely however that in 1967 as well as in 2009 the word "slavery" would conjure up very stiff resistance in the public at large even if it was of the most altruistic kind. A possibility not specifically mentioned in the report, however, was the dovetailing of this alternative with the space research alternative offered in the field of economics. A recruitment system along the order of the military draft could be installed and used to provide the personnel that would be engaged in the colonization of the moon, for example, as well as the personnel needed to construct and operate the space research alternative. Such a recruitment system could be operated on a quasi-voluntary basis as is the military in the US in 2010. This is to say that it could come equipped with the ability to offer large sign-up bonuses to relieve immediate problems, and above average compensation during the term of service, even for life, as would normally be the case in any type of colonization program. In terms of altruism, this approach would be at least comparable to the existing military system in the United States. In the long run it also has the benefit of garnering the support of the public at large for the need for government; and would also be capable of transferring the anti-social behavior of suppressed classes and minorities into a form of patriotism for a world government on Earth. Whether or not either the space research alternative or the above recruitment alternative is feasible is a matter of speculation. There does not seem to be any reason that some type of massive space research program could not be established, but whether or not outer space colonization is possible would depend on the technological breakthroughs generated by the program. This in turn would determine the need for a recruitment plan.

There may also be similar possibilities available that were not considered by the report. It was the conclusion of the report that these alternatives would be seen by the public not as a replacement of the war system but rather as an attempt to sustain the war system and be counterproductive to the goal of a general peace. These two alternatives are what have been suggested by the report as replacements for the non-military functions of the war system in the operational aspect of the political arena.

The report also offers four alternatives to the war system in relation to the motivational aspect of the political functions. First, it is suggested again that the creation and intentional intensification of an environmental threat could act as an alternative to the war system. No program of a specific nature was set forth by the report in relation to this alternative. Several possibilities readily come to mind. A nuclear release could be staged in the form of a series of accidents. The actual accidents associated with the Love Canal incident, as well as that associated with the meltdown at Chernobyl, would lend credence to this scenario. It would also be possible to create a few accidental spills of crude oil such as that of the Valdez that would pose a substantial threat to the environment.

The most effective, however, might be to intentionally intensify the threat of climate change, whether a real or as a creation in the media, which could be used to produce the sense of immediate danger. Such a manipulation of the public in the modern world seems to have little chance of long term success as long as the public has access to broad and diverse sources of information. In short, this alternative would fail to generate the needed credibility to make the threat effective.

Second, it is supposed that the creation of a new religion, or at least a new system of mythology, could stand as an alternative to the war system in terms of motivation. The new religion, or mythology, would need to be specifically targeted at generating a feeling in the public that secular government was essential and that their personal wants must be sacrificed to the public good. This alternative is not entirely out of the question as most existing religions play a very strong part in supporting the secular governments under which they operate; as well as, inculcating a strong sense of duty in the individual to accept and obey the established authority. The report concludes that the artificial creation of such systems is not likely to be feasible considering the slow evolution and accidental arrival of the existing models and it is dismissed as unpractical.

Three, the creation of some sort of public blood games is suggested as an alternative. Again, nothing of a concrete nature is offered by the report in support of this alternative. It is imagined, however, that they would act in much the same way as the gladiatorial games did in ancient Rome. That is, they would be used to displace the anti-social behavior of the part of the public that felt themselves deprived. Some would say that professional sports in the US today are already fulfilling this same function. However that may be, it is certain that such games would be clearly seen by the public for what they were and that they could not be used to create a motivation in the public to support any existing system of government.

Four, it is also suggested that some combination of the three alternatives set forth above could be created to replace the war system. Again no concrete program is set forth to explain how this combination would look or how it would operate.

The report dismisses all the alternatives offered in the political arena as impractical as replacements for the functions played by the war system. They placed the most hope in some type of alternative that would incorporate the altruistic slave alternative but did not offer any suggestions as to what it might contain. In short, the report appeared to be unable to come up with an alternative to the war system in the political arena. This would tend to the conclusion that a general peace was not a possibility.

Five, in the area of ecology the only alternative offered by the report was a system of controlled eugenics. Under the proposed system of eugenics the production of children would be rigidly restricted to in vitro fertilization. This restriction on birth would be accomplished by a pollution of the water supply and the necessary food supplies with contraceptive drugs. Pregnancy would be strictly controlled by the government's selective administration of the antidote for the contraceptives used. Not only could the balance between the number of humans and their supplies be maintained but the quality of the race could be "improved". This would of course require the "scientific" choice of those who would be allowed to have children based upon some model of improvement. The only problem that the report found with this alternative was that it could not be introduced until after the general peace had been established. There are however several obvious problems with such a program. The logistics of supplying the contraceptives without the knowledge of the public, that is, the use of the water and food supplies appears to be impractical. It also seems unlikely that such a tactic could be maintained in secrecy and once known would be unacceptable to the public at large. There are also the problems of who would decide on what constituted an "improvement" of the species, who would decide on how such an improvement was to be implemented, and lastly, how to determine which couple, or which female, would be most likely to bring about this improvement. In short, the whole alternative represented by eugenics seems to be impractical from both a political and scientific standpoint.

Six, in the area of the cultural–scientific arenas the report flatly denies that any alternative to the non-military functions in these areas exist. One may remember that the main non-military function of the war system in this field was to supply a system of values to the culture and to provide a system of motivation for scientific improvement. The report states that the culture, at least as represented in the fine arts within the US, was operating without a system of values and that no replacement for the war system was needed. The report concluded that the motivation for progress in the scientific and technological arenas would no doubt be furnished by either the space research program or the expanded social welfare system as a matter of course which would eliminate the need to specifically plan for it.

The report had now completed its task of setting forth the alternative programs that it was aware of and of judging them on the basis of the criteria it had set forth in relation to their potential of success. Although the authors of the report did not set forth a specific conclusion concerning their findings it appears that they assumed that a general peace was neither possible nor desirable as of 1967. A general peace was not possible at that time, according to the report, mainly because the necessary planning and research had not yet taken place concerning the non-military functions of the war system. They were essentially unknown and if known misunderstood by those in the know. As a result the alternatives available were all superficial and unstructured and would lead to even greater ignorance and misunderstanding if instituted. A general peace, even if possible, would be undesirable because it could not be instituted without a massive destabilization of the existing social institutions. The extent of the expected destabilization in the opinion expressed in the report was that it would lead quickly to the total collapse of civilization as then known. As a result in the view of the report only two possibilities remained with any level of reality. First, a system of planning could be implemented for the slow conversion of the war system into an alternative system that would minimize the level of destabilization when the general peace was instituted; or second, that a system of planning could be instituted that would aim at a more efficient use of the existing war system to execute its non-military functions. The report saw the latter as the most likely under the circumstances that existed in 1967. At any rate, the report concluded that a general peace and the establishment of a world government under the conditions that existed in 1967 was merely the wishful thinking that normally accompanies a utopian vision of the future.

It would appear that in the four decades since 1967 neither of the programs suggested by the report has been instituted. Instead, the war system has been left to an uncontrolled evolution and no sustained planning has been given to the establishment of a general peace. Early in the report the unplanned initiation of a general peace was painted as the worst case scenario. Would the same lack of planning and structure be just as dangerous today?

Obviously, many aspects of the world environment have changed substantially since 1967. It is likely that revisiting the questions raised by the report would lead to very different results. Let us begin by assuming that the non-military functions of the war system exist and that the current social institutions that exist are in fact what are called the war system by the report. There is at least a question as to whether or not the war system exists (as a coordinated, conscious social institution), let alone that its non-military functions exist. As stated earlier it is not really important whether or not either exists in relation to the purpose set forth within this work. It is interesting regardless of whether or not a general peace is both possible and desirable. For this reason we will revisit the major questions raised by the report. Depending on the conclusion reached a determination will need to be made concerning the best method of instituting a general peace. As a result the same areas of concern will be treated as in the report but from the standpoint opposite of the conclusions offered by the report. That is to say that the areas of concern will be looked at from the viewpoint that both general peace and a world government are feasible and possible.

First, it will be necessary to take a detailed look at the economic field as it probably is the most important one in relation to the modern world. We can begin with two generally accepted premises; one that a very substantial portion of most national budgets are expended on military institutions or what the report calls the war system. This is particularly true if we also take into consideration the internal policing activities of nation states; two, that the economic effects of this level of expenditure extend very deeply into the overall functioning of the global economy as a whole. This being true there is no doubt that the rapid unplanned dismantling of the various military institutions world-wide would result in very massive economic dislocations. One need only look at the economic destabilization that occurred after World War II in the US with the rapid and essentially unplanned demobilization of the country's military. The result was a rapid increase in prices, unemployment, and material shortages. Earlier the same type of unplanned, or at least uncontrolled, expansion of the US industrial capacity was partially responsible for the economic destabilization that resulted in the Great Depression. World War II is seen both as partially responsible for ending the Great Depression and for bringing about the circumstances which eventually led to the planned economy of today. It is, therefore, very likely that any attempt to establish a general peace will require that an extensive amount of prior planning take place to limit the destabilization expected in both national and global economies. Indeed, it is likely that the success of a general peace and any attempt to establish an effective world government to support it will be dependent on this planning for their success. The planning required will have to be concentrated in two separate areas. First, a plan will need to be in place for a verifiable total disarmament, or dismantling of the existing military institutions, that is to say, the war system. This planning will not only have to include the disbanding of all military weapons but also a verifiable system for destroying the weapons and any toxic waste associated with them. Both the disarmament and the destruction of the existing weapons will require the institution of an agreed upon international inspection system. Second, the planning in this area would also have to include a plan for the immediate replacement of the military budgets involved with equally effective spending in other areas of the economy. In this area the report provides us with an alternative system that would be very effective especially if carried out under the auspices of an effective world government. That alternative is the establishment of a massive welfare program aimed at bringing all of the world's citizens up to a relative parity in terms of their standard of living. I do not believe that there has ever been an estimate made of the amount of money, manpower, and materials that would be needed to accomplish such a project. Assuming the project not only included personal outlays for unemployment compensation, disability compensation, old age pensions, and other entitlement programs, but also infrastructure projects such as roads, bridges, sewer systems, water systems, etc. the outlay of money, manpower, and materials might not reach completion within the 100 years predicted by the report. It is certain however that some type of effective supervisory institution would be needed to compile a list of the needs, the location of these needs, the method of eliminating these needs, and to provide the supervision necessary to execute the plans made. It is likely that this would, in fact, be the major function of any effective world government, i.e., its oversight powers. The question is whether or not this alternative to current military spending would be effective in preventing the expected economic dislocations. For it to be successful it would have to replace the current military systems expenditure of monies, manpower (in terms of employment), and materials (in terms of the amount of industrial products consumed). Using the United States as an example, the alternative system would have to replace nearly 25 cents of every dollar of revenue taken in by the federal government, it would have to provide about twelve million jobs (both for those currently serving in the military or who provide services to the military), and several billions of dollars in industrial products (to replace those now produced exclusively for military use). Using the current estimates that abound in various places for only the repair and maintenance of the existing infrastructure in the US the expenditures of the military could be replaced for a substantial number of years. If substantial portions of the existing military budget were to be diverted to a worldwide development of infrastructure the replacement value might exceed a couple of hundred years. Regardless, serious planning must take place concerning the conversion of existing military expenditures before a successful institution of world peace and world government can occur.

With the completion of what the report calls the capital outlay phase of the welfare system two new expectations are to be met. First, are the continued expenditures for the maintenance of the infrastructures created under the first phase, which would include not only the maintenance of the physical structures, but also the staffing and stocking of such institutions as schools, hospitals etc. The same would be true of the bureaucracies created to implement the various social programs such as social security, national health programs, and all the other safety nets established to maintain personal standards of living. Second, assuming that the report is correct in its assessment that at this point the welfare system will become a part of the normal supply and demand system a determination will need to be made as to what effect that has on the economy as a whole. The fact that the welfare system would become a part of the normal supply and demand system, in the opinion of the report, was important because the normal supply and demand system is not subject to arbitrary government control. As a result the welfare expenditures could no longer be manipulated to control the fluctuations that from time to time affect the economy. We have seen that these expected fluctuations include depressions (the most serious), recessions, stagflation (the most persistent), and imbalances in world trade. Assuming for the moment that existing military expenditures are actually used in a conscious fashion to control these fluctuations it is still questionable as to whether they would be effective in performing this function. It is true, at the very least, that since 1929 there has not been another great depression although there have been a number of examples of recession, stagflation, and severe trade imbalances. It is also true that there have been a number of police actions, that is, the Korean conflict, the Viet Nam conflict, and the expulsion of Iraq from Kuwait which have essentially coincided with the fluctuations in the national and global economies. It is however debatable as to whether or not the above conflicts were used consciously to control the economy in addition to their obviously political nature. It is very likely that the supposed non-military functions of the war system in the economic arena are truly a mythological construction made to prove a point. The only connection with reality is the fact that dismantling the war system would in fact create serious economic dislocations that would have to be addressed by some effective alternative system of expenditure. The effects of the war system therefore are not truly non-military but rather specifically military. In the modern world the unplanned failure of the existing national welfare plans would be as disruptive as the dismantling of the military institutions and would arguably create more human suffering.

It would appear that a plan that would immediately come into effect upon dismantlement of the existing military institutions, that is the institution of a plan for the relative equalization of worldwide standards of living would create an environment whereby the expected economic dislocations could be avoided. The long evolution of a program aimed at the relative equalization of the standard of living worldwide would likely consume all the expenditures that would have been expended under the military institutions, even assuming a continuation of the limited shooting wars of the last seven decades, for a minimum of twenty five years and possibly a maximum of one hundred years if not more. There is no real need for arbitrary government control, at least in the sense presented by the report, as the war system does not have any non-military functions in this area. Economic fluctuations, that is, economic stability, does not appear to be tied any more strongly to military expenditures than to any other ordinary economic factors such as global trade. I do not pretend to know with any degree of confidence the causes that are involved in economic fluctuation but I am sure that those who do understand them will come up with creative ways to control them when and if the need for them arises. The real problem that faces the citizens of the world today is whether or not those who rule them can be made to see the wisdom of creating the plans that would be needed to insure the success of a general peace and an effective world government. This is true even if, as some believe, the world is ruled by a relatively small number of people who control the global economy.

Second, in the political arena the report clearly assigns the non-military function of the war system the task of producing an environment that promotes both the acceptance of the public and the public's need for government as well as the motivation to obey the commands of that government. The war system accomplishes this function by putting before the public the constant need to be prepared for war. It can be assumed that the most pressing part of this need is to prevent the external invasion of one country by another. It is this fear of disturbance in the public confidence of its safety that the report places the public's motivation to accept government and to obey its commands. Secondarily, it also includes the public's fear of loss due to internal insurrection that is civil war, riot, labor disputes, or other forms of violence. Lastly, the domestic military functions include the control of crime (internal policing, i.e., the enforcement of civil and criminal laws within the national boundaries). It is likely that the public acceptance of the need for military and para-military institutions is directly related to the fear they feel for their safety both from external invasion and internal harm. Granting that the public has accepted the war system as a means of protecting their individual rights, it still remains to be seen whether or not the government has actually used the war system for that purpose. It would appear that the public's expectations have not been met. In the US, for example, the public has been presented with an almost constant involvement in some type of international policing action since the close of World War II as well as constant civil unrest related to labor disputes, civil rights, and environmental issues. If the war system was intended to allay the fears of the public against violence to their person, it has failed in the United States. In addition, the 1970 anti-war protests, the various civil rights protests, and the general repugnance of the public against violent crime clearly indicate that the sense of fear has grown, not diminished.

Three, the report states the following concerning the war system and the non-military functions of the war system in relation to sociology: "The permanent possibility of war is the foundation of stable government. It supplies the basis for general acceptance of political authority. It has enabled societies to maintain necessary class distinctions, and it has ensured the subordination of the citizen to the state, by virtue of the residual war powers inherent in the concept of the nation-state. No modern political ruling group has successfully controlled its constituency after failing to sustain the continuing credibility of an external threat of war."[1]

There is really no justification for the argument presented above. While it may be arguable that the threat of external invasion, internal insurrection, and criminal violence may all have played a part in the public acceptance of the need for government it is not the only source of this need. It may not have even been the most important of the factors that occasioned the public acceptance of government and the consequent willingness to obey the demands made by government. There have been equally powerful forces, if not much more powerful forces, in creating a public acceptance of governmental authority. Some of these include religion, ethnic identity, geographical boundaries, language and customs. All of these individually and certainly in combination represent equally important motivations in individuals for the acceptance of the need for social organization and the obedience to governmental regulations and commands. One need only look at the modern use of an ancient Islamic concept to see the truth in the above statement. The modern concept of Jihad as used by the current fundamentalist sects of Islam will clearly indicate the importance of religion, for example, in the winning of acceptance and obedience of those who are Islamic in belief. It is clear that the threat of external invasion (whether by another nation or by insurrection) still exists and represents one aspect of the public awareness of the need for government. It is also clear that the continued appearance of civil war, riots, and other challenges to internal security also support the public awareness of the need for civil government. If a general peace is possible and desirable what is available to replace the fear of violence to the person as a motivation for acceptance of government and obedience to governmental commands?

One such alternative may be that offered by Francis Fukuyama in his book "*Trust The Social Virtues and the Creation of Prosperity*"[2], under this alternative Fukuyama suggests that the acceptance of government, and the willingness to obey the commands of government, is built up from a generalized socialization process that is dependent upon a large array of intermediate organizations that exist between the family and the government. Fukuyama labels this slow accumulation of acceptance of authority as social capital versus ordinary capital. The ability of any given individual to accept a position within a group and to trust those that make the rules for the group is totally dependent upon his experience in trusting beyond the immediate or extended family. This trust is directly related

---

1 *Report from Iron Mountain on the Possibility and Desirability of Peace*, The Dial Press, Inc. 1967, New York.

2 *Trust The Social Virtues and the Creation of Prosperity*, Francis Fukuyama, A Free Press Paperbacks Book, Simon And Schuster, 1996.

to the ability of the individual to spontaneously organize into groups that include non-family members. Historically such groups have been religious, civic, or political organizations with all being related by the fact that they were voluntary. This is to say that the creation of the organization as well as the obedience given to its rules and regulations were voluntary. In Fukuyama the main emphasis was placed on the evolution of large scale economic institutions such as the massive corporation rather than in government per se. It is according to Fukuyama no fluke that those countries that contain the largest deposits of social trust are also those that have been the most successful in developing the large scale of economic organization needed to compete in the global market. He also relates the ability to trust non-kin in the development of social and economic organizations with the ability to evolve governments based upon representative democracy. Organizations based upon this concept of social capital tend to operate with less specific definitions of property rights, contracts, and litigation. In each of these societies, the high level of trust generated by this ability to cooperate with strangers was the result of being able to participate in non-family organizations holding an intermediate place between family and the state. These organizations allowed a large number of people to maintain a shared moral structure, a shared interest within the society at large, and generated high levels of trust between the members. When industrialization came on the scene, according to Fukuyama, the high level of trust between strangers in these societies made it possible to easily develop the large corporate organizations needed to cope with the industrial revolution.

Fukuyama did not detail the relationship between high levels of social capital (trust of strangers) and the success of various political organizations, except to denote that liberal democracy seemed to be one of the major components of success in the global market, and that high levels of social capital seemed to be necessary to sustain a successful commitment to liberal democracy. From his definition of social capital however it would seem to follow that a successful democracy would require a high level of social capital resulting in a minimal defining of property rights, a minimal setting forth of contract rights, and a minimum use of the judicial system to enforce contract rights. It would also seem to convey the sense that a maximum of acceptance and obedience would be voluntarily granted to government.

In relation to a general peace and the establishment of an effective world government it is imperative that an understanding of what supports social capital be developed. Fukuyama sets forth several factors that he considers to be of great importance in the evolution of social capital. First is the importance of education which begins with the learning process, provided by the nuclear family. The political organization, at all levels, must support this value system by doing everything in its power to insure that the education received is of the highest quality. This assumes, in turn, a large degree of support for education from religious and secular institutions alike within the society. In turn it also requires that the state, the religious and secular institutions, and the individual invest a great deal of effort in the support of the nuclear family as the basis of all education values. The nuclear family however is only the first step in the process of accommodating any individual to an acceptance of sociability. It is also necessary that the highest levels of government do nothing to hinder the evolution of a dense layer of socializing institutions intermediate between the family and the state. It is at this point that individuals voluntarily interact with strangers (those that are not members of their immediate family structure) and learn social trust. These institutions come in all manner of descriptions such as public and parochial schools, professional organizations, civic organizations such as the Lions, the Chamber of Commerce and others. Each of these organizations has one common element, with the possible exception of the public schools, they are voluntary. They are voluntary in the sense that belonging brings with it a cost in time and effort that is voluntarily accepted by those who join.

Second, it is important to remember that Fukuyama demonstrates that social capital or trust can both be lost and created. However, he points out that it is much easier to lose this capital than to create it. He shows that the early conscious effort of the French government, for example, to destroy the then existing dense layer of intermediate institutions in French society resulted in the low level of social capital found there today; while on the other hand, the conscious sponsoring of such organizations by the state, as in Japan, has led over time to one of the highest levels of social capital.

Third, the report has set forth the concept that the military institutions represent one of the best socializing agents in society. That is to say, the military institutions take the most anti-social elements of the population and through the application of military discipline return them to society with a high level of sociability. In reality it appears that the military institutions, especially during times of shooting wars or police actions, return the members in a worse condition than they found them. At the very best the military institutions appear to be inefficient in socializing their members. In addition, the war system is based upon the forced acceptance of the need for authority and the forced submission to the demands made by that authority. Social trust, on the other hand, is based upon the voluntary recognition that all organizations require leaders or rulers and that obedience to the demands of the rulers, within limits, is a voluntary cost of membership.

Fourth, liberal democracy historically has sponsored the creation of a dense network of intermediate institutions, supported by the evolution of a quality education, and by the promotion of the voluntary nature of membership (citizenship) in the state. As a result liberal democracies tend to have a high level of social capital at hand, not only for the development of economic prosperity, but also in relation to the acceptance and obedience to the dictates of the state.

In the political arena the war system should be replaced with the conscious effort to establish as dense a network of intermediate institutions as possible with the benefit of producing a high level of social trust over time. It appears that the best form of government for the creation of social capital in this manner is a liberal democracy.

Four, in the ecological arena it must be remembered that the non-military functions of the war system were to arbitrarily create a method whereby the human population could be kept within the limits of the supplies needed to guarantee the survival of the species. It would appear that what was meant was that an occasional shooting war of a size necessary to eliminate excess human population would need to be created or intentionally fought. It is true that the destructive capability of historical wars has kept pace with the increasing rapid growth of the human population. Therefore, World War II was the most destructive in terms of cost in human lives of all wars fought up to that time. Since World War II however shooting wars of that type have been generally avoided rather than instituted. The size of the human population currently, coupled with the selective inability of certain areas to sustain that population, points to the conclusion that the war system has failed in the area of ecology. It is more likely that starvation, disease, accidents, natural catastrophes, and other causes have been much more effective over historical time in controlling the human population in relation to the supplies available. Even the loss of life occasioned by World War II would probably pale in comparison with the loss of life from the other sources listed above for the period between 1900 and 1940. The real distinction, however, between war and the other causes listed is that shooting wars specifically target the portion of the population that is most fertile. The removal of a large number of productive males and females from the underlying society such as was the case with the former Soviet Union during World War II creates a long term reduction in the total population growth. Any real decrease in one society, however, is more than compensated for by the uncontrolled growth of populations in other nations. The report appears to have reacted to the real fear of nuclear war that existed in 1967. It is likely that an all out nuclear war would have reduced the worldwide population in a manner compatible with the non-military function of the war system claimed by the report. In the modern world of today it would appear that this function if it exists at all will be replaced by the unintended results of industrialization. The continued pollution of the environment if not controlled will eventually lead to the predicted results promised from the concept of climate change. The continued pollution of the environment will not only lead to massive loss of human life but also to a massive reduction in the amount of supplies available to insure the survival of the species. In the worse case scenarios the extinction of the human species is predicted in relation to the loss of supplies to sustain life under the concept of climate change.

The report suggested that the war system could be replaced by a controlled system of eugenics. This alternative was eventually dismissed as being ineffective. In our case the continued pollution of the environment must be faced and eliminated before planning can begin concerning the control of human population growth. This is a real problem currently, that is, there are specific areas of the world where the growth of population has outstripped the supplies available to support it. In these areas there is massive loss of life due to starvation, disease, and other natural causes. Although it is possible that the whole world considering the current population may still be small enough to be sustained by available supplies it is believed that we are rapidly approaching the point of population saturation. If this is accurate then the institution of a world government would also include the delegation of the power to outline a program or programs which would effectively control future population growth to maintain a balance between population and supplies. Currently it seems that the most confidence is being placed in voluntary birth control through the use of birth control drugs. This has to date not been particularly effective. I do not pretend to have the knowledge of what might be effective as well as voluntary in this area. What is certain is that some type of program or programs will need to be developed on a worldwide scale to solve this problem in the short term. It would seem likely that a program incorporating education, contraceptives, and legalized abortion may be the most effective method available currently if allowed to operate on a voluntary basis. This program would be overseen by the world government to insure uniformity of application and the testing of results in terms of their success in obtaining the goal. The program would however be most effectively administered by the national and local governments. In all cases the most important long term aspect of the program would be continuing education and the most important short term goal would be easy access to contraceptives and competent legal abortions. It is important to note that in all countries where the birth rate has fallen below that of the death rate, that is, where the birth rate is negative this result has been obtained on a voluntary basis. This is not to say that tax incentives, subsidies, and other means should not be used to motivate individuals to control the number of children they produce. In the end it seems that any type of eugenics program would be out of the question as repugnant to the general sensitivities of the public.

Five, in the area of cultural–scientific endeavor the report was unable to offer any real alternative to the non-military functions of the war system. This may have been the result of the fact that the war system has never played an important or key role in establishing the value system within any existing culture; and was only one of many motivations that led to the progression of science especially its technological aspect. As with the non-military functions of the war system in economics there is a color of truth in the statements presented in the report. There is no doubt that many artists whether painters, sculptors, or writers have obtained their fame and fortunes from the portrayal of scenes of war or the leading personalities of the warriors. There can also be no doubt that many of the technological inventions were the result of the need to solve some military problem or that they were soon incorporated into the military organizations. This, however, is much different from saying that the value system of any specific culture, or the only source of motivation for the evolution of science and technology, resides in the functions of the war system. Indeed, it is likely that the war system does not provide any of the values of cultural life but rather uses the values that it finds to support the goals of the military institutions. The same seems to be true of the motivation provided for the progress of science and technology, that is, the war system uses what is created but does not provide any or only an insignificant amount of the motivation leading to that creation.

The Report from Iron Mountain purports to be a serious analysis of whether or not a general peace is possible and desirable. It is certainly open to debate when the content of the report is detailed whether or not it was successful in its attempt. Regardless of its success it does raise some very important questions concerning the types of problems that would arise with the establishment of a general peace. If the report has done nothing else it has focused attention on the fact that war has always been a major component of human existence. It concludes that any attempt to establish a general peace is a utopian dream of the most futile type. As a result the report concludes that a general peace is neither possible nor desirable. Our analysis of the report, the war system, the alternatives to the war system, and the other aspects of the report led us to the opposite conclusion, that is, that a general peace (including the institution of an effective world government) is both possible and desirable. The current work will approach the problems presented by the report with arguments that will set forth methods concerning the most viable method of creating a world government based upon liberal democracy. The choice of liberal democracy as the form of government is based upon the theory presented by Francis Fukuyama, i.e., that liberal democracy seems to be a necessary component for the creation of social trust. It is also the form of government that seems most likely to contain the flexibility to successfully cope with the expected dislocations that will occur with the institution of total disarmament, that is, the dismantling of the military institutions. An attempt will also be made to outline some of the processes that have developed within liberal democracy (The United States) that tend to nullify its ability to create social trust and the flexibility to handle unforeseen consequences or problems. The concept of world government as a whole is utopian in the sense that the existing system is to be broken down and replaced with a new system. The system of nationalism is to be dismantled to a significant degree and is to be replaced with a supranational system.

Before turning to the base arguments it is necessary to offer some preliminary thoughts concerning the structure of the current political environment. There can be little argument against the supposition that all forms of government have been created and maintained by the use of force. This is certainly true of the so-called empires of the Akkadians, Egyptians, Chinese, Assyrians, Persians, Romans, and others. It is equally true of the so-called religious empires of the Christians, Muslims, Hindus, and others. There are sometimes exceptions allowed for the governments established by the Sumerians, Athenians, and the United States, among others. These exceptions, however, do not seem to be accurate when one considers the history of these governments. It is this constant use of force to create and maintain societies that lend credence if any can be given to such theories as those presented in the Report

The establishment of a general peace, and a world government, does not, therefore, require advanced planning in relation to the replacement of the non-military functions of the war system but rather advance planning for the replacement of the war system itself. The first step of course would be to establish whether or not the world is ready to accept the concept of a world government that would bring about world peace. If the world should decide that it has no interest in either then so be it as neither is possible without the desire to have them. This decision could be made by the simple expedient of asking for a "yes" or "no" vote on the question using the current United Nations General Assembly. If the result of the vote is yes then the next step would be to decide whether the establishment of world government would proceed through a reform of the existing United Nations Charter or by the process of calling a constitutional convention for the creation of a new government. This would include a system whereby the new constitution or the remodeled U.N. Charter could be ratified and put into effect. The creation, at least in theory, of an effective world government is that simple.

However, the conditions that would have to be met before the creation of a world government or the conditions that would have to be met immediately after the institution of the government are anything but simple. For example, a total disarmament would need to have been either accomplished prior to the creation of the new government, or a binding agreement would have had to have been concluded outlining total disarmament upon institution of the new government. This only recognizes the fact that a world government, regardless of its form, cannot be successful or effective if the current world military environment remains in place.

Assuming all of these hurdles are successfully overcome then the world government would begin its evolution into whatever it will become just as every other government that has maintained itself over a substantial period of time has evolved. The National governments will also undergo the same process of evolution as they would now exist in a completely different environment both socially and politically. This would include a breakdown of the current prejudices that accompany the system of nationalism. As Fukuyama has suggested the most effective means of breaking down local prejudices seems be in the creation of social trust. If nations are looked at in total as large family structures then social trust is built by bringing the citizens of each nation (family) out of its dependence on the nation as a family. Currently nations are supported by such commonalities as language, geographical proximity, customs, religion, etc. The solution is to extend these commonalities to intermediate organizations that include them all, as well as, those found in other nations until it is common for all citizens to recognize their humanness. As will be pointed out there are some developments within the framework of liberal democracy that tend to prohibit the institution of such social capital building organizations.

The question at this point in time is still whether or not the people of the world will accept the responsibility for creating and maintaining an effective world government and a general peace. It is certain that there will be resistance to any change that disturbs the emoluments of those in positions of power. This is certainly true of nations such as the United States which currently hold a large portion of the military capability that exists in the world. It is also true however of the individuals, whoever they may be, that control the political destiny of the individual nations.

CHAPTER 2. GENERAL CONSIDERATIONS CONCERNING LIBERAL DEMOCRACY

One way in which an effective world government could be established is set out in this chapter. It is, of course, assumed as a basic premise that there has already been a decision on the part of the existing nations to create a world-wide government. Beyond this nothing is assumed to have been agreed upon and what follows is more of the nature of suggestion than a presentation of actual possibilities.

Initially an attempt will be made to show that the conditions that existed in 1790 were comparable to those that exist today in relation to the creation of a liberal democratic republic. The similarities will be highlighted by the circumstances that faced the thirteen states and the modern circumstances facing the world's nations. That is to say, it will be shown that the reasons that led the citizens of the thirteen states to reject the Articles of Confederation of the United States of America and to ratify the new constitution of the United States are comparable to the reasons that exist for the rejection of the current Charter of the United Nations and its replacement with an effective general world government. It can be shown that the U.N. Charter is as ineffective in obtaining the goals intended to be accomplished as the Articles of Confederation were for obtaining the goals intended for them. The rejection of the Articles of Confederation, coupled with the ratification of the new constitution, created the United States of America. It is hoped that the rejection of the United Nations as an effective world organization will lead to the creation and ratification of a constitution creating the United Nations of Earth or some similarly named entity. In order to follow the process that could occur in the creation of the world government a detailed look at the process that led to the creation of the United States will be undertaken.

It took something on the order of eleven years of operation before agreement was obtained both among the ruling elite of the thirteen states and those in positions of leadership in the Confederation that the federal government created by the Articles of Confederation had failed. The agreement to replace the existing government was universal the question remained however concerning what should replace the Confederation. A convention was called to determine how the Articles of Confederation would be reformed to create an effective general government. In the end, the convention scrapped the Articles and produced a radically different constitution.

Before this Constitution could go into effect, it had to be ratified by nine of the thirteen states. The ratification process stirred up a considerable amount of debate over each of the articles contained in the Constitution. This debate is highlighted by the production of a series of articles written by Alexander Hamilton, John Jay, and James Madison which became known as the Federalist Papers. In these articles the main arguments for and against the ratification of the Constitution were set forth. The Federalist Papers also set forth in general terms the arguments that favored the use of a republican democracy as a form of government. In our case the form of government argued for in the Papers is synonymous with our terminology, i.e., liberal democracy.

It is being suggested here that the Constitution of the United States be used as a detailed guide in the writing of the constitution intended to replace the existing U.N. Charter. This being so, it is also suggested that the arguments that favored liberal democracy and the specific articles of the US Constitution would still apply. Before entering on a specific discussion of the content of both the US Constitution and the Federalist Papers, however, let's consider whether or not there were any special conditions that existed in 1789 that made it possible for the US Constitution to be successfully initiated and which would prohibit the same thing from occurring today.

One continually mentioned factor in the success of the US Constitution is the homogeneity that existed in the population of the then existing thirteen states. This factor is seen to be the most important aspect of the success of the early United States. It has, indeed, become an enduring myth not only outside but also inside the United States. Like all myths it has within it a kernel of truth. There can be no doubt that the ruling elite in the early United States all spoke the same language, that all of them practiced the same religion (Christianity), that they all came from similar backgrounds in regard to customs and manners (they were to a large degree all from Western Europe). They also had all been involved in the late colonial governments and had participated in the drafting of the state constitutions after the war for independence had been concluded. When one looks closely, however, the homogeneity was largely insignificant. Religion, for example, while all within the bounds of the term Christianity, included a vast number of protestant sects, Catholics, and others. This diversity in religion was as heterogeneous as that which existed in Europe and could have caused the same problems or wars as in Europe. There were also serious disagreements between the various regions of the country in terms of customs, manners, education, and other social distinctions, and in many regions English was not the primary language.

The experience of the ruling elite however did give the founders of the US Constitution several areas of common belief. Their education, for example, brought them to a clear understanding of the purposes that were to have been accomplished by their predecessors in Europe. During the Great Rebellion and later in the Glorious Revolution in England the mainstays of democratic political ideology were formed. These events had occurred less than one hundred years prior to the creation of the United States. It was during these events that the concepts of separation of Church and State, the sovereign power of the people, the use of widespread suffrage, and representative democracy were initiated. It was also during these events that the antagonism between merchants, industrialists, and the working class were first felt in relation to the developing industrial revolution. The emotions generated by these distinctions led to the beheading of a monarch, the tyranny of Cromwell, and the establishment of an over-zealous parliament. Added to these basic elements of their education were the results of over a century and one half of experience of self-government as English colonies. In essence the thirteen colonies were treated as independent nations closely confederated with Great Britain. Therefore, for nearly 150 years the ruling elite in the colonies had been operating under the principles of a republican democracy. Therefore, the real homogeneity that existed in 1789 was based upon a common belief in liberal democracy, the operation of a free market economy, and the separation of Church and State (the prohibition against the establishment of a state religion). Today whatever homogeneity that exists is to be found in the common acceptance, especially since the fall of communism, of liberal democracy, liberal economics, and a dependence upon science and technology. The first two are comparable to the circumstances that existed in 1789, the common political heritage of the thirteen colonies, and their belief in the operation of a free market system. The latter however has no counterpart in the early experience of the US, but was very quickly to become an important factor in the evolution of the US system of government. Some writers such as Francis Fukuyama contend that the world as a unit has already come to the stage where liberal democracy is the only viable form of government in existence. He would also contend that liberal economics which today does not include the old concept of a free market system has already progressed to the point that it is the only form by which a national economy can compete in the globalization of the market place. Lastly, he would contend that the world today regardless of the form of government or the actual content of the global market is committed to a real dependence on the continued development of science and technology. These factors are best explained by the motivations that direct what I will call "consumerism". The term consumerism will be limited to the expression of the desire of each individual to maximize his or her standard of living based upon the accumulation of material goods. The most glaring example of the power of consumerism is the fact that the drive to obtain higher standards of living based on the availability of goods is credited as the reason for the Soviet Union's failure. It is also credited with the worldwide failure of right wing totalitarian systems that fail to take heed of their citizens demanding consumerism. The success or failure of any system to comply with the demands of consumerism is judged by its ability to favorably compare to the standard of living found in Western Europe, the United States, and Japan. It does not appear, at least at this date, that much attention has been paid to the developing theocratic systems. The most potent of the theocratic systems seems to be that of Islam. It is likely, however, from the turn of recent events that even secular Islam will be judged by its ability to produce a favorable comparison with the "west" in terms of standard of living and the distribution of material goods to individual citizens. Whether or not Islam will be capable of adapting its system of faith and government to the demands of consumerism remains to be seen. The general wisdom concludes that Islam will be unable to cope with this demand just as other forms of totalitarian government have failed. The conclusion reached by writers such as Fukuyama is that the world generally appears to be ever more dependent on the continued evolution of modern science and technology. The evolution of modern science and technology in turn seems to be best supported and promoted by liberal democracy coupled with liberal economics. The three together are seen to be responsible for the highest standards of living and distribution of material goods now in existence. At the very least, there can be no doubt concerning the constant acceptance over the last 400 years, especially the last eight decades, of a significant number of nations for a liberal democratic form of government.

Today a large number of the world's nations are operating under some form of liberal democracy coupled with an economy based on liberal economics. Unfortunately this movement has been marred at times by two factors. On the one hand, liberal democracy has in some cases been imposed from the outside by force such as in Germany and Japan after the conclusion of World War II and in Afghanistan and Iraq today. On the other hand, a number of nations that have tried to institute liberal democracy have failed to maintain that form of government in part due to corruption from within. In these cases as in Africa, Southeast Asia, and Central and South America the democracies established were slowly converted to military dictatorships or some other form of totalitarian government. Even with these interruptions however the number of nations operating under a liberal democracy has continued to increase especially since the end of World War II. These facts would lend a great deal of credibility to the view that liberal democracy is in theory if not always in practice the most viable form of government in existence today at least in the light of the requirements of consumerism.

It must be pointed out however that liberal democracy does not come in just one type of government. In some nations such as Germany, Japan, and France liberal democracy takes the form of a true national government. This is to say the general government holds all the power, duty, and responsibility of sovereignty and delegates whatever power, duty, or responsibility that is held by any lower levels of government if any. As in any liberal democracy, at least in theory, all the power resides in the people who delegate this power through their representatives to the general government who in turn delegate some of the power to the lower governments. In other nations such as the United States and the Russian Federation, the liberal democracy takes the form of a republic. Under this form of democracy, all power again putatively resides with the people. The people, however, through the drafting of a constitution, have delegated the power to both the general government and the lower levels of government. In the case of the United States, this includes a delegation of power to both the general government and the governments of the fifty states. All lower levels of government such as city, town, village, county, etc, are operated by a direct participation of the people, that is, as a true democracy. In some nations such as Great Britain the power delegated to the general government is concentrated in the House of Commons (parliament), through the election of a prime minister and his party who attempt to concoct a coalition of members to arrive at a majority of votes. In each case these nations all have a unique understanding of what it means to be dependent upon modern science and technology, to operate as a democracy, and to have an economy that is based on liberal economics. The US and Great Britain can be considered the earliest models of modern liberal democracy. The systems evolved in nations such as Germany and Japan can be seen to be as different from each other as both are from either of the early models. The early models, of course, are as different from one another as they are different from Germany or Japan.

It is also very important to remember in what manner writers such as Fukuyama relate modern science to American-style liberal economics and democracy.

In their theory, modern science does not stand alone although it is the motor that drives the modern world. For the most efficient and effective evolution of modern science to occur, according to the theory, modern science must be supported by liberal economics and liberal democracy. Modern science has as one of its major goals the rational division of labor. Liberal economics supports this goal by providing the structure that will most effectively use this division of labor from the standpoint of cost. This support includes the ability to use the economics of scale, the development of highly flexible labor-intensive industries, a global market, and rational regulation to prevent abuse. Liberal democracy with its commitment to the rule of law, the protection of individual human rights, and concern for the sovereign power of the people provides the means whereby modern science and liberal economics can be regulated to provide for the satisfaction of the needs of all the people. In short, modern science and technology provide the tools for the most varied production of the products demanded by consumers. Liberal economics, they assert, provides the conditions under which these products can be most cost effectively produced, and American-style liberal democracy provides the regulation that insures the best possible distribution of these products to the greatest number of people. It is on the basis of this theory of modern social needs that Fukuyama and others are led to believe that it is the only viable means of satisfying the demands of the world's population.

It is far from clear, however, if this theory is the only one that can provide these benefits. China, for example, is not what they mean by a liberal democracy, but its economy is based largely on liberal economics. This hybrid system is currently very competitive in the global marketplace and their economic growth is impressive. The Chinese have created a hybrid form that is competitive with the system set forth above. Of course, China is committed to the development of science and technology and liberal economics.

Other models exist and many styles of government have been tried, each with its own varying emphasis on concentrated privilege and power versus broader rights, including the right to higher education, decent living standards, and others.

It is also possible to challenge the concept of liberal democracy in specific cases. For example, Howard Zinn in his work *A People's History of the United States*[1] questions whether or not the US has ever operated as a liberal democracy. It is likely that his analysis could be applied to any liberal democracy now in existence. Zinn attempts to show that the US was created for, and has continuously

---

1 *A People's History of the United States 1492–Present.* Howard Zinn. Harper Collins Publishers, 2003.

operated for, the benefit of the small wealthy elite. This of course would make the US an oligarchy rather than a democracy.

Zinn claims that the US Constitution was drafted by a group of men who collectively controlled most of the wealth of the new nation. The Constitution was written to guarantee that their existing property rights (wealth), would be protected (not taken or distributed to those less fortunate), and that they would be in a position to control those whom the "people" elected to represent them. There is no question that the fifty-five men who were appointed to serve at the constitutional convention were either very wealthy in their own right or were closely associated with those who were very wealthy. It is also true that, to a large degree, they incorporated into the Constitution the prejudices of their class. This, however, is saying something much different from the accusation that those who drafted the Constitution intentionally attempted to install a government for their exclusive benefit and to hide the fact that they were doing so. Only those who could afford the time and expense of spending three or four months drafting a constitution were available to serve.

This has been the case since the first government was formed and continues to be the case today. It is just as likely that they included the protection of property rights and some degree of control of their class in the Senate in good conscience as it was a part of the understanding of a liberal democracy at that time. It is true, however, that the method chosen to ratify the Constitution was at least one step removed from the vote of the people and most likely two steps. The Constitution was ratified by the state legislatures who in turn were elected as the representatives of the people. This brought the ratification process at least one step removed from a direct vote by the people. The state legislatures were made up of persons who had both the time and leisure to provide public service. They were in fact of the same class as the people who drafted the Constitution and who promoted the ratification of the Constitution. This is the cover of validity assumed by Zinn in his representation or at least accusation that the Constitution represents the conscious efforts of an oligarchy to protect their vested interests. It is of course a matter of speculation as to whether or not a conscious conspiracy was being perpetrated or whether an honest attempt was being made to create a liberal democracy as that term was then understood. It is the opinion of some historians that an honest attempt was being made to create a liberal democracy as that term was then understood; but the compromises that were obtained to make ratification possible were subject to specific class interests and prejudices as could well be expected. Zinn's theory however is one interpretation of the constitutional process that must be kept in mind when a decision is made to use, or not to use, the US Constitution as a model for the document that creates a world government.

Zinn continues his work with the delineation of major events in US politics. He concentrates on such issues as slavery, labor unrest, the various wars that the United States has embroiled itself in, and the civil rights movements such as the suffrage movement, the abolition movement, the abortion movement, and others. All these events or movements are consistently treated in the traditional historical rendering of the US experience. In each case, however, Zinn presents the concept that the solution to the event or movement was found in the least amount of compromise on the part of those in control of the government necessary to quiet the social unrest and to keep the wealthy elite in power. In terms of the individual suffering that resulted from these events or movements and the slow success of their aims Zinn presents a very credible theory. However, if one takes each issue, i.e., event or movement and continues to follow it from its inception to the position it occupies today a very different picture forms. For example, when one looks at the history of the movement involving the right of citizenship within the US the following picture appears. Initially citizenship under the Constitution was only granted to white males who held in their procession a stated amount of property (wealth). This was the standard at the time for citizenship in any country including those that were considered to be democracies. This definition of citizenship excluded all women, all those in servitude (indentured servants), all people of color (African and Native Americans), and all free white men who did not own enough property to qualify. Under this initial system it is fair to assume that maybe as low as ten percent of the population qualified to be citizens at least in the sense of the ability to vote and to hold public office. What is ironic about the initial system is that everyone living within the borders of the thirteen states was considered to be a citizen when it came time to tax them and to draft them for military service. This is one of the most important factors Zinn claims as the proof of his theory concerning the establishment of an oligarchy from the beginning of US history. However, it must be remembered that this was the common practice in every nation of Western Europe and was the common experience of the colonists. It probably did not seem at all out of the ordinary that the Constitution should be drafted in such a manner and, in fact, was probably seen as complying with the dictates of liberal democracy as then understood. The fact that this system was not challenged for some fifty or sixty years would tend to confirm this hypotheses. The last one hundred and forty years however have seen an ever broadening definition of citizenship at least in the case of the right to vote and hold public office. During this period of time the initial system created by the Constitution has been completely dismantled to fit the evolving realities of the political environment. As of today every citizen of the US who has obtained the age of eighteen has the right to vote and the right to hold public office with very few exceptions. Even those who are not citizens, although they do not have the right to vote, have obtained a significant array of rights under the laws of the United States. The same type of favorable expansion of human rights can be followed in every issue raised by Zinn. In the end, it is not the fact that individuals had to fight and often to suffer severely to gain the rights that are now accorded to them; or the fact that there have been times when the wealthy and the poor have taken different sides on an issue that is being debated, but rather, the fact that democracy has been flexible enough to accommodate the changes required by the evolving political environment that is most important. In place of the intentional attempt of the wealthy elite to maintain control of the govern-ment it is just as easy to substitute an evolving ideal of what constitutes a liberal democracy. It is certainly likely that the poor and the underrepresented did find themselves suffering and being killed in disproportionate numbers in both civil unrest and war as this has been true every since government was first created. What is of importance is that under the system created by the US Constitution those who suffered and who died in disproportionate numbers had recourse for their grievances. They were not only able to bring to the attention of the public their specific grievances; but they were also able to obtain satisfaction of many of their demands. During most of human history the poor and underrepresented have been the dumping ground for the dregs that have been left over from so-ciety when all others have been satisfied. It is amazing to this author that the US represents after two hundred years plus of operation one of the few places on earth that the needs of the poor and underrepresented are even considered. This is especially true when it is taken into consideration that the wealthy have always been capable of monopolizing political power for their benefit. Although this pattern has not yet been completely broken it has been seriously bent by the principles of democracy practiced in the US over the last two centuries. Re-gardless of the validity of the interpretation offered by Zinn his work has clearly shown that it is possible to question the motives that seem to operate within a system claiming to be a liberal democracy. He also points out the fact that a liberal democracy has the capability of being manipulated by a hidden faction operating as an oligarchy or tyranny. As Zinn concludes there is no substitute for the constant vigilance of the people over their own rights; which may have been the real point of Zinn's theory of an oligarchic conspiracy.

Chapter 3. What Form Should a World Government Take?

What type of constitution is likely to result from the convention envisioned in Chapter 2? The establishment of a world government within the demands of a continuing dependence on modern science supported by liberal economics (in this context the rational regulation of the global market and inter-nation trade) and liberal democracy (in this context to provide for the rational distribution of sovereign power to insure the most efficient obtainment of individual human rights) is the general criterion. Are there more than one or two existing systems that could be used as a model for the convention in drafting this constitution? It would appear that there are at least two, that is, the republican Constitution of the United States, and the parliamentary system in use in Great Britain.

Both are liberal democracies, one of the purely national type and the other of a republican type. Both have a long history of successful operation within the parameters established above. In our context, however, the real advantage of the United States over Great Britain is that the system found in the US is based upon a written document rather than a piece-meal evolution. Great Britain began its path towards liberal democracy in 1215 with the signing of the Magna Carta by the English Monarch. It has continued to evolve into the current parliamentary system every since with an occasional lapse into other forms of government along the way. There are of course other forms of government which could be chosen by the convention such as an oligarchy, an aristocracy, a monarchy, a theocracy, and so forth. As has been pointed out these forms of government, while at one time expressing legitimate claims for recognition, have over the last couple of centuries greatly diminished in use. It is suggested therefore that the convention be limited to the creation of a world government based upon the principles of a liberal representative democracy. If the US Constitution is used as a guide as is suggested here the convention will be limited to the creation of representative republican democracy. The Constitution of the early United States was consciously created by fifty-five men who knew exactly what they had in mind. It was the first time in history that a government had been created in writing and submitted to those who would be ruled by it for their approval. In today's world a better procedure could not be implemented to guarantee the success of the experiment. The convention, if it uses the US Constitution, will need to make a decision as to whether or not the amendments that have been added should be incorporated into the new constitution. Some will argue that the contents of these amendments are politically specific to the historical situation of the United States and should be relooked at in light of the conditions that face the new government. Others will argue that they should be incorporated into the new constitution and voted on during the ratification process. The convention during its debate will undoubtedly make this decision. It may be that they will decide to incorporate some of the amendments and leave others for later debate dependent upon the necessity of solving similar problems. For the sake of argument, the proposed draft of such a constitution set forth herein will incorporate most of the amendments to the US Constitution into the body of the proposed constitution of world government.

In addition, the argument can be presented that the US as it exists today represents the most successful example of fulfillment in terms of consumerism and its demands. The US has one of the highest standards of living in the world today even when one considers its poorest citizens. In fact, the very concept of "consumerism" is to a large degree determined by a country's comparison with the United States. In this sense, the US can be considered the most successful in promoting the growth of modern science and the most supportive of liberal economics and liberal democracy — these being the standards that people like Francis Fukuyama use to judge a countries chance of success in the 21st century.

The question stills remains as to whether or not the results obtained by the US can be transposed to any other environment than that which existed in the historical United States. The best that can done, at least initially, is to set forth the circumstances that existed in 1789 when the US was created and compare them with the environment that exists today. Some of the factors that have been traditionally listed as the most important in allowing the success of the early US are as follows. First, that the population of the thirteen states was very homogenous, i.e., they spoke the same language, they largely came from the same background in relation to customs and manners, and that they all were of the same religion. Second, the people of the US had some one hundred and fifty years of practice in self government of a democratic form. Third, that the people of the US were essentially isolated geographically from the most powerful nations on earth. These factors are of course important but the question is whether or not they are vital. In relation to the first of the traditional factors it is fair to say that it only applies to the ruling elite both in the Confederacy and in the states. There were three and one half million people in the United States in 1790. Of this number only a small proportion were considered to be citizens. All women and children were excluded from citizenship, at least, in terms of being allowed to vote or hold public office. All African-Americans and Native Americans were excluded from citizenship as were all indentured servants. All white men who did not own a minimum of property, either in land or an equivalent, were also prohibited from voting and holding office although they were considered to be citizens. Therefore, it is fair to say that the ruling elite probably represented something less than five percent of the total population. When one also factors in the willingness to hold public office, coupled with the wealth and leisure to do so, the total ruling elite may have been as small as one or two percent, or some 35,000 to 70,000 individuals. It is certain that this group of the population did have the type of homogeneity that is spoken of above. As concerns the second factor it is also true that the same individuals, or their ancestors, were the people that represented the one hundred and fifty year experience of self-government first as colonies and second as a confederacy. As to the third factor it is true that Great Britain, then one of the strongest nations on earth, could not effectively fight a war on the North American continent and prevent the loss of the thirteen colonies. The new US, however, was surrounded by very strong nations, i.e., the British were still in the Ohio Valley and Canada, the French were still in the Mississippi Valley, and the Spanish were still in Florida and Louisiana. In addition, Great Britain still held control of the seas. Regardless, the early US leaders realized that they were relatively safe from external invasion by European powers and were mainly worried about these countries supporting Native Americans in their wars with the United States. All of these factors therefore did exist in 1789 and did contribute significantly to the success of the early United States. The question is whether or not the fact that they do not exist in relation to our concern for world government is vital. As concerns the first factor it would appear that the experience of the United Nations and the experience of the European Union both clearly point to the fact that in the modern world the lack of a common language, common backgrounds in customs and manners, and a common religion will not prevent the establishment of effective communication. With today's technology it is possible to provide simultaneous translation of oral communication as is the case in the United Nations. It is also possible to quickly translate any written documents that might be involved. It is also a surety that the success of the world government is dependent upon the acceptance and promotion of the diversity that now exists in all these areas. As to the second factor it is true that there are a significant number of nations and peoples on earth who have not had the opportunity to live under a democratic government, and who, therefore, have no experience with that form of government. It is also true that the majority of the nations on earth have had at least some experience at operating under a democratic form of government. Even those who have not are currently experiencing the operation of modern science and liberal economics. It is likely that an effective world government would not, at least initially, need to be composed of nations solely ruled by democratic forms of government. As to the third factor one merely needs to point out that no one spot on earth is geographically isolated from the danger of attack by insurrectionists or any other intentional use of violence. It is hoped that an effective world government would lead to the elimination of this shortcoming. One may conclude therefore that the lack of these factors that helped the US succeed will not in the situation faced by the creators of a world government prevent its success.

The fifty five men who came together in the constitutional convention in 1789 brought with them a shared set of ideals due to the homogenous nature of their backgrounds. One of these ideals was a republican form of government. They had a very specific type of republican government in mind. They were familiar with the republican form of government found in ancient Rome. This type of republican government is known today as the national republic. Under this form the sovereign power remains with the general government. For example, when Rome formed its republic the tribes that were incorporated into it such as the Latins, the Sabines, and others were forced to give up their citizenship in these tribes and to become citizens of Rome alone. In short, as various tribes and peoples were made citizens in the Roman Republic they lost the sovereignty they had in their own tribes or countries. Whatever powers, duties, or responsibilities remained with the various tribes or peoples were those that were delegated to them by Rome. The delegates to the convention were also not driven to form a republic of the kind formed between Scotland, Wales, and England which in many ways was comparable to the US under the Articles of Confederation. The delegates to the convention saw Great Britain more as a monarchy which at the time it still was than a democracy even though some degree of democracy had already evolved in Great Britain. Because of the historical situation it is unlikely that the form of government operating in Great Britain was even considered. The experience formulated from the eleven years of operation under the Articles led to the final consideration. The convention was aware of the general wisdom that what had been the greatest defect in the Articles was a lack of sovereignty. This fact coupled with the fact that all of the state constitutions had established republican forms of democracy favored the creation of a republican form of government for the union. The first debate in the convention revolved around how the sovereign power would be delegated and how much of this delegated power would be given to the general government. The debate began with the democratic principle that all power resides in the people. The only effective way for the people to delegate their power is through a written constitution. Using a written constitution allows the people to grant, deny, or reserve specific powers to any level of government they see fit. Any power not delegated or denied specifically to one or another level of government would automatically be reserved to the people. If a power was not specifically delegated to the federal government, or denied to the states, it is considered to have been reserved to the people or to the states as their representatives. In order to accomplish this division of power the convention found it necessary to construct a republic.

A second common ideal brought in common by the delegates to the convention was religion. All of the delegates whether they were personally committed or not had been brought up within the tenets of Christianity and most had been raised in Protestant denominations. In 1789 the public mind was still keenly aware of the religious persecutions that had brought them to the colonies in the first place. Most of the persecutions that had been perpetrated stemmed from the existence of state sponsored religions in their countries of origin. The common ideal that they carried with them was that all individuals should have the right to practice religion in any manner they saw fit. Freedom of worship as it was understood by those in the convention did not mean that religion would not play a part in government; but rather, that government would be denied the power to create a state religion. It would also deny the government the power to make public service dependent upon the taking of a religious oath. Indeed, it is very likely that all of the delegates to the convention felt very strongly that religion was necessary to produce an orderly society. Religion had up to that date always been the main source of ethical and moral teachings.

A third common ideal revolved around the issue of economics. The delegates had for the most part been brought up in the English tradition that followed the teachings of Adam Smith. Under the system founded by Adam Smith the economy was to be left to evolve directly from the free play of the market forces. In short, Smith advocated the least amount of government interference with the economy as possible in the form of regulations. Smith called for some regulations, within each nation, for the control of international trade, as well as internal trade, but essentially the market was to operate unrestrained. Most of the regulations would be related to supervising the value of money, the use of a standard weight and measure, and a procedure for the settlement of disputes. The only real internal regulation that was seen as necessary was to put the general government in control of import and export duties. This system had slowly evolved over a period of nearly two centuries before Adam Smith was able to systemize it in economic theory. Included within this system was the sub-system of imperialism. Under this system it was internationally recognized that every nation was entitled to be protected in its possession of whatever areas of the world that it could control. Nation-States were also given, at least in theory, the quarantine of the freedom of the seas. They were also given sole control over their own ports and the ports of their colonies in relation to the establishment of import and export duties and restrictions. Lastly, each nation was given sole control over its internal home market, which, of course, also included all its colonies. These rights were incorporated into the US Constitution having been recognized as imperative by those who attended the convention. For example, the federal government was given the sole power to establish import and export duties and to regulate the trade between the several states. This latter was probably intended to be essentially limited to the providing of a forum for the settlement of any disputes that might arise between the states. The US at the time of the Constitution did not have any colonies so that was not specifically treated in the Constitution but there was an interest in the Ohio and Tennessee Valleys. In this area the federal government was given sole jurisdiction for all transactions involving US territories.

From a general point of view those who took the lead in the US in creating the Constitution were all educated in the civilization that had evolved in Western Europe over the last two or three centuries. The principles that underlay this civilization were in many cases well developed intellectually such as the concepts of liberal economics and liberal democracy but had not yet become of much practical importance. That is to say, although the theories were well known, and had been much debated, there was only one country that had taken any real steps in establishing these concepts in reality. The same cannot be stated for modern science. By 1789 the process known as the industrial revolution had already begun and progressed to a significant degree in Great Britain. It would not be long before it spread to the European continent and to the United States. The rapid growth of scientific thought, and its counterpart technology, had led to a general questioning of authoritarian traditions and had created an environment suitable to creativity. It must also be remembered that the United States was composed of very diverse elements if one takes into consideration the whole population. There were approximately half a million African-Americans and a quarter of a million Native Americans living within the borders of the United States. They both of

course spoke different languages than English; had different religions than Christianity; and different customs and manners than those among whom they lived.
In 1789 they were at the very bottom of the economic and political ladders. The
US was also roughly divided into three distinct regions. The "Old Northeast"
that included New York, Pennsylvania, Massachusetts, New Jersey, Connecti-
cut, Rhode Island, and Delaware and was the commercial and financial capitol
of the country. This region had also been able to develop a significant start in
industrialization. The "old South" included Maryland, Virginia, North and South
Carolina, and Georgia. This region was largely based upon an agricultural tradition coupled to the system of slavery practiced in the early United States. Those
at the upper end of the economic scale had tended to adopt a rather aristocratic
attitude and in terms of educational level were comparable to the same economic
level in the Northeast. The "northwest territories" which included most of the
Ohio and Tennessee Valleys were essentially frontiers. They were rather sparsely
populated and were dependent upon both the south and northeast for material
products. Those areas in turn were quickly becoming dependent upon this region for natural resources such as timber. Although not yet formally incorporated
as states they had been ceded by the states to the federal government with the
imposition of the Articles of Confederation. This latter area was the only one in
direct contact with the British, French, and Spanish colonies; as well as with
the independent Native American nations. The sole exception was Georgia who
was in contact with the Spanish and Native Americans settled in Florida. The
tradition or myth would have one believe that the early US contained little if any
diversity however the reality shows that a great deal of diversity existed and is
still an important part of the US system.

A look must now be taken in relation to the difference of opinion that existed
upon ratification of the Constitution in regard to the status of the federal government. One side of this issue can roughly be designated as those who wanted and
fought for a strong federal government. The other side can be roughly designated
as those who sought to keep the federal government limited in relation to the
power of the states. The contention between the two sides would be labeled as
the fight over states rights. The most prominent spokesmen that led the fight for
the constitutional convention and the ratification of the Constitution also led the
fight for a stronger federal government. As a result they were termed "Federalists". Those that led the fight for limited federal government were mainly located
within the state governments and took the label "anti-federalists". The federalists included such men as George Washington, John Adams, John Marshall, and
Alexander Hamilton. The anti-federalists included such men as Thomas Jefferson,
John Calhoun, John Jay, and Aaron Burr. The base of power for the federalists

was located in the northeast while the base of power for the anti-federalists was located in the south. Although the western territories were split on this issue they tended to back the federalist position on most issues. A balance of power so to speak existed between these two competing philosophies for the first thirty years of operation under the new Constitution. The federalists between 1790 and 1802 held the executive branch of government under George Washington and John Adams. The legislative branch however held a majority of representatives that favored the anti-federalist position. The Judicial branch was in the process of being formulated during this early period but at the very end of the period John Adams as he was leaving office packed the Supreme Court with justices who adhered to the federalist position. Of greatest importance was the appointment of John Marshall as the chief justice. He was to hold office until 1834 and rendered arguably the most important decisions ever given by the Supreme Court. As a result the tide slowly turned in favor of the federalist philosophy.

It can be claimed that the two hundred year evolution of the US has completely altered the conditions that existed in 1789. There are now approximately three hundred million citizens in the United States although it is probably true that only about the same percentage of the population is in a position to hold office. The rights and duties of citizenship in relation to the franchise and holding of public office has been expanded to include all adults who have obtained the age of eighteen regardless of their color, gender, or religious preference. The use of voting restrictions such as property qualifications, literacy tests, poll taxes, and others have been essentially eliminated. Yet in the last presidential election less than fifty percent of those registered to vote actually voted. If one was to look at state and local elections the percentages of those who actually vote is even less. There are now fifty states rather than thirteen and at least four rather than three distinct regions. The population of the US is one of the best educated, wealthiest, and most religious in the world. The US is now also highly diverse in the languages spoken, the number of religions practiced, and in customs and manners. Lastly, the debate over the federalist and anti-federalist philosophies has been completely decided in favor of the federalist point of view. The question that must be settled in relation to the modern US is whether or not it has become a national democracy rather than a representative democratic republic. It is difficult to find any activity that is carried on by the state or local governments that is not affected by federal regulations, financing, or other control. Yet, it seems to be true that the powers that still remain with the state and local governments are not powers that have been delegated to them by the federal government. If those who were responsible for the creation of the United States could return today they would not be able to recognize the federal government. It has grown to a size that would not have been capable of being imagined in 1789. The federal government is capable of intervening in areas of daily life that would probably cause them much concern. It is for this reason that it is important that we maintain a strict separation between the ideals that are represented in the constitution and those that are represented by the evolution of the US outside the Constitution. It is only the ideals that are incorporated into the US Constitution that are of concern in the establishment of an effective world government.

When one analyses the parliamentary democracy that arose in Great Britain a much different picture emerges. The most notable difference involves the fact that democracy in Great Britain was a matter of development over many centuries. As a result democracy in Great Britain is the result of a series of unplanned events that led in combination to the parliamentary system that exists today. For example, Great Britain was a traditional monarchy until 1215 A.D. A traditional monarchy was a form of government, at least in Western Europe, where the monarch held its right to rule directly from divine choice, that is, the monarch held the right of secular rule through delegation from the Catholic Church. In 1215 the English Lords were able to limit the sovereign power of the monarch to a degree through the signing of the Magna Carta. Under this document the leading aristocrats or nobles were delegated the right to establish a House of Lords that had the power to consult with the monarch on legislation that effected them. They were not elected by the people, but rather appointed from among their peers. In all essentials the sovereign power remained with the monarch in all parts of Great Britain, that is, England, Wales, and Scotland. Although power remained with the monarch it became obvious that the monarchy could not be maintained without the support, both in a physical sense, that is, militarily, or financially without the aid of the leading nobles. Representation in the House of Lords was restricted to only the wealthiest of nobles, that is, the largest of the landowning nobility. This state of affairs continued for some period of time. With the development of modern science and liberal economics however another class of citizens began to demand representation in legislation that affected their interests. This class of people consisted of the lesser nobility, large manufacturers, large financiers, and large merchants especially those who controlled the trade with the growing colonial empire. They also soon became indispensable to the monarch in terms of paying for and maintaining the large armies needed to maintain the colonial empire. These elements were eventually admitted to the House of Lords giving them a voice in the government. At a later date the general class of manufacturing and commercial interests coupled with the growing power of the urban areas began to demand representation in the monarchy. The House of Commons was created to accommodate these interests rather than absorbing them into the

House of Lords. The major difference between the House of Lords and the House of Commons was that the representatives of the House of Commons were elected to office rather than getting representation automatically by class membership. This was a specific recognition of the growing power of the large cities and towns. Over the last several centuries the House of Commons has slowly usurped all the real power vested in both the monarchy and the House of Lords both of which are now more or less figureheads of government. The House of Commons now provides for the nomination of the executive branch through a majority system within its membership. That is to say the person who is able through fluctuating coalitions between the various parties in the House of Commons to garner the majority vote will be installed as prime minister. These coalitions are either conservative or liberal in political philosophy depending upon the type of coalition that is formed. The prime minister is able to maintain control of the executive branch only as long as he or she is able to maintain the confidence of the coalition that put them in office. The judicial power of the parliamentary system also resides in the hands of the House of Commons who nominate the judges. The parliamentary system of democracy that exists in Great Britain, Canada, Australia, and India appears at first sight to be more tied to the historical development of a specific nation than that of the United States. All of the countries that currently are operating under this system were for a substantial period of time either directly under the control of Great Britain, e.g., India or populated by people that came directly from Great Britain such as Australia and Canada. The parliamentary system of democracy does not seem to lend itself well to the role of guide for the establishment of a world government. It is of course possible that a world government established on the basis of a parliamentary form of democracy would operate in a suitable fashion; but without the requisite experience with the operation of such a government it would be very difficult to institute, especially on the basis of a written constitution. It should be taken into consideration that this form of government seems capable of operating efficiently within the context of multiple political parties, and in its abilities to resist the influence of well organized and well financed interest groups. In addition, it has shown itself adept at adapting itself to the needs of a diverse population in regard to social, economic, and cultural conditions. It would be wise to make an in depth analysis of why parliamentary government has these capabilities while it seems that the republican government of the US does not. This concern will occupy some of our attention as we proceed.

There are two other forms of government that need to be looked at as potential candidates as guides for the establishment of world government. The first that will be looked at is the government that is currently in place in the Republic of China. The second will be the government that is commonly associated with those nations that practice Islam.

First, the Republic of China classifies itself as a communist government. The leading tenets of traditional communism (as established first in the theories of Karl Marx, and then later in the Soviet Union as a practicing form of government) are the following. One, that all property is public, i.e., is owned by the state in its corporate capacity. Two, that the state through its ownership of the means of production will guarantee the equal distribution of all wealth within the society. Three, that the state will stand as the guarantor of the equal rights and duties of every individual of which the society is composed. It is apparent that the China of today, and the Soviet Union of the past, do not, and did not, comply with these tenets. Since its introduction in 1949 the Republic of China has slowly allowed the reintroduction of a limited amount of private enterprise, or as we have called it liberal economics. Although the Republic of China, as with most democracies, claims to be making great strides towards the equalization of wealth it still remains a largely class segregated society. The Republic of China, as the Soviet Union before it, in reality only provides equal rights under the law to those who are members and actively support the communist party. This does not, and never has, included the majority of the population. The trend in the Republic of China, although it may be a short term phenomena, seems to be towards a larger acceptance of modern science, an expansion of the use of liberal economics, not only internally but also in relation to entry into the global market, and a relaxation towards a growth of liberal democracy. If this trend continues it is likely that communism will fail in the Republic of China as it did in the Soviet Union. Although communism must be regarded as important in relation to the establishment of a world government it is likely that it will not contribute significantly to the actual government formed.

Second, the system that is associated with those nations that espouse Islam is very complex. It is currently just beginning to come into its own in regard to modern politics. Some countries such as Saudi Arabia and Thailand are still governed by monarchies that hold to the faith of Islam. In other countries such as Turkey and Egypt there has been a solid attempt to introduce secular government based upon liberal democracy but coupled to a state religion, that is, Islam. In other nations such as Sudan and Somalia the country is ruled by Islamic dictatorships. In others such as Iraq and Afghanistan the form of government has been imposed from the outside and is technically a democracy but in reality chaos. Lastly, some countries such as Syria and Iran are controlled by a true theocracy controlled by the Islamic clerics that lead the Shi'ia sect of Islam. It is safe to say that all these different forms of Islamic government can be held to be theocracies, which by definition means that they are totalitarian in nature. It goes without saying that the only people for which this type of government is appropriate is those that have belief in Islam. There could of course be secular arms established in Christianity (the religious right), Buddhism (the Lamaism of Tibet), or any other of the existing religions. Religion plays a powerful role in many countries throughout the world including the United States. It is likely that it will also play a very important role in any world government that is formed. This, however, is not the same as saying that the world government should be formed as a theocracy. In reality the only way that a theocracy could be considered is if all the peoples of the earth adopted the same religion which in today's environment seems incredible.

Within both of these systems the populations ruled by them appear to be putting significant pressure on the rulers to liberalize their governments. They are seeking better educational opportunities, more personal freedom to choose their way of life, and they are demanding an increase in their standard of living and material comforts. China has already shown signs of relaxing its internal policies to comply with these demands. The same is true for the nations that accept Islam with the exception of those who are ruled by Islamic fundamentalism. Islam faces the further challenge of worldwide disapproval of the use of violence as a political tool. It would however be a mistake to attempt any type of forced conversion of the existing Islamic governments as the experience in Afghanistan and Iraq clearly indicate. It is likely that both communism and secular Islam will fail to adapt to the needs of modern science especially its dependence on liberal economics and liberal democracy. As a result they will be forced by the people ruled by them to alter their form of government.

The conclusion therefore is that the most reasonable guide in the formation of a world government is liberal democracy. The most appropriate form of liberal democracy in the attempt to establish an effective world government appears to be a representative democracy formed on the principles of a republic. In turn the most likely choice for guidance in the creation of this type of government would be found in the US Constitution. The Constitution was intended to create a representative republican democracy. As the US developed under this Constitution it consistently supported the growth of modern science, the evolution of liberal democracy, and the support of liberal economics. If writers such as Francis Fukuyama are correct in their analysis of the current world environment then just such a government is demanded. The purpose to be served by the government created by the Constitution was to provide a means to solve the problems that were too large to be solved by the individual states. These included protection from external invasion and internal insurrection, the settling of disputes between the states in a peaceful manner by an independent, unbiased arbitrator, and the protection of individual human rights. The same would, of course, would be true of a world government. A world government would also be expected to provide the means to solve such global issues as environmental pollution (including the manmade contributions to climate change, if any), the conservation of natural resources, and the regulation of the use of outer space and cyberspace as well as the threat of pandemic disease. There are other arguments that could be offered but those that have been presented make a rational case for the use of the US Constitution as the guide for establishing a world government.

Chapter 4. Historical Considerations for the Use of Democratic Republican Principles

What would a world government patterned after the US Constitution look like? What type of responsibilities, or goals, would be assigned to such a government? What powers would be given up, or retained, by the individual nations that would compose the union? What type of duties and responsibilities would be demanded of the citizens of a world government? What would be retained by the citizens in regard to their individual rights? These, and many other, questions need to be answered to the satisfaction of both the nations that now exist, and to the people at large, if ratification of such a government is to be expected. The same was true in the case of the Constitution that was drafted to create the United States. The Federalist Papers was one means by which all of these questions were laid before the states and the people when seeking ratification of the Constitution. We began with the conclusion that any government, regardless of its form, must meet three basic goals. First, all governments must have a degree of willingness of the people to accept it as their ruler. Second, every government must have some degree of willingness on the part of its population to preserve it. Lastly, all governments have to have a degree of willingness in the people to obey the laws passed by the government and to perform the duties demanded of them by the government. Without these three basic goals being met even the most stringent use of force will not for long succeed in sustaining the government in question. It will be assumed, therefore, that the world government contemplated herein has succeeded in gaining the acceptance of its citizens; that the citizens are willing to sustain the government and they are willing (within reason) to obey the laws and perform the duties demanded of them. On the other hand, the citizens can reasonably expect that the world government will attempt to provide for their general welfare, and protect their individual human rights. Beyond these basic qualifications all else is a matter for debate and compromise.

The debate cannot begin until the prospective citizens of the new world government are presented with the choice as to accepting or rejecting the contemplated project of establishing a world government. This choice is essentially one that has three parts. First, a choice must be made concerning the desirability of a world government. There are two different ways that this can be done. A direct vote of the people can be taken, but this would be cumbersome and inefficient to say the least. It would be more practical if the vote was taken by nation through the appointed representatives of each nation now members of the United Nations. Provisions would also have to be made to include any nations, or people that are not members of a nation, to cast their vote, either individually or through the United Nations. This vote could be assigned either a two-thirds or three-fourths acceptance level to proceed. Second, assuming that a favorable vote was obtained in the initial vote then a mechanism for the construction of the world government would need to be set up. It has been already suggested that the most effective way to accomplish this would be to set up a constitutional convention. This would include electing or nominating the personnel to conduct the convention. Third, assuming again that the convention was called and that a proposed constitution was drafted a mechanism would need to be set up to ratify and put the new constitution into effect. This could be done in the same manner as the initial vote, or it could be done by the individual votes of the Nations under the laws appropriate to each nation. In the case of the United States Constitution the whole process took something on the order of two years to complete from start to finish. It is to be recommended that the process be kept as simple as possible to avoid unnecessary delays. The initial vote should be a simple yes or no vote to a question worded something in the following manner: "Do you want a world government to be established?" The second part of the process would require that each nation appoint the personnel they wanted to serve at the convention. It is possible that a committee selected by the full United Nations would then select from those representatives the personnel that would actually serve at the convention; or each nation might be allowed only one delegate. Again the goal would be to keep the process as simple as possible and yet capable of conducting day-to-day business at the convention. The last vote again would be limited to a simple yes or no, that is, either the nations would or would not ratify the constitution as written. A reasonable amount of time would need to be given for each nation to debate the content of the constitution and to make a decision concerning ratification. It is recommended that a time limit of three years be placed on the debate concerning ratification. If not ratified within three years, the constitution would fail to go into effect.

The early US could be used as an example of how the constitutional convention would be staffed. Under the procedure used by the US, the state legislatures nominated the persons that they felt were most competent to fulfill the task at hand. The result was the nomination of fifty-five men to sit in the convention. If the same procedure was used in our case, and each nation selected only two delegates the number of people serving at the convention would be roughly four hundred. The question arises here whether or not this large a number would create a situation in which day-to-day business in the convention could not be conducted effectively. It is, of course, imperative that the size of the convention be limited to a number of delegates that can reasonably be expected to conduct business. Assuming a positive vote has been obtained concerning the establishment of a world government the size, and method of choosing the delegates to the convention, should be determined prior to the actual call for the convention. This problem was not faced by the early US and will be handled on the basis best deemed fit by the world's nations. It is suggested that some system be created by which the delegates can be selected from those nominated by the various nations. It is also recommended that the actual number of representatives to the convention be kept as low as deemed feasible, although the number probably would not need to be as low as the fifty five selected by the early United States. The convention would be called after the selection of the delegates and be seated in a place deemed to be neutral, such as Geneva. It could also be stipulated, if deemed necessary, to put a time limit on the convention for producing a proposed constitution. Depending on the size of the convention this time limit could be as short as six months or as long as one year. Once the proposed constitution has been drafted then it would be the most efficient to submit it to each nation for ratification, again using some type of timeline for completion. The amendment procedure in place for the U.N. Charter could be used to determine the ratification process; however, that procedure requires the unanimous vote of all five permanent members of the Security Council. Although all five of these nations, for practical reasons, may need to ratify the new constitution it would be unwise to allow one of them to derail the ratification process prior to reaching a majority determination by the rest of the nations. In relation to the time period allowed for debate and ratification of the new constitution a procedure should be created to allow the collection of questions that might arise. These questions could then be debated under the procedure selected and answers returned to the appropriate nation. It is suggested that the original convention be kept in operation during the ratification process for this purpose if deemed necessary. It is also necessary to consider in advance what procedure will be followed should the constitution be ratified without the participation of the key nations mentioned. In other words, would the world government go into effect anyway with the expectation that these nations would later join the union or not.

Before a proposed constitution can be written, as mentioned earlier, the convention must debate what would be expected of an effective world government in terms of duties and responsibilities. The powers specifically delegated to the general government would be determined by what would be needed to accomplish the expected duties and responsibilities. In theory, the very least that would be expected of an effective world government would include the following. First, the general government would have the duty and responsibility for maintaining peaceful relations between the nations that belonged to the union; as well as, with nations that did not become members, if any. Second, the general government would be expected to establish a judiciary capable of resolving any disputes that arose among members on the basis of finality. This would, of course, include disputes that might arise between members and any non-member nations, and between the general government and any non-member nation. This responsibility to peacefully resolve disputes by law would extend not only to the member nations in their corporate capacity; but would also devolve down to the level of their individual citizens. Third, the general government must be capable of passing all laws necessary to execute the duties and responsibilities delegated to it and to enforce such laws against both the member nations and their citizens. Fourth, the general government must have the physical power, in terms of a military presence, to maintain peace between itself and any non-member nations; as well as, having the capability of policing any common areas of activity, such as the open seas, outer space, or cyberspace. Fifth, the general government must be capable of independently financing its day-to-day operations and any unusual expenditure that might arise.

In order to accomplish the first duty, the general government must be given the power to create a military institution capable of coping with any individual nation, or group of nations, that might attempt to attack the general government, or any member nation. If a total disarmament is carried out in connection with the establishment of a world government, the military structure needed will be minimal in comparison with the US arsenal of today. The duty in this area would not only included the prevention of external invasion by member nations upon other member nations, but also by non-member nations invading member nations; and the suppression of internal insurrections when beyond the ability of the affected nation to handle. This will undoubtedly be one of the most sensitive issues facing the convention, especially if total disarmament has not yet occurred, which it in all likelihood will not have. In short, for this power to be effective in the hands of the general government all existing nations would have, at the very least, have signed an agreement to conduct total disarmament procedures prior to the convention. Any disarmament agreement would, of course, include a procedure for verification of disarmament, and procedures for the destruction and disposal of all nuclear, biological, and chemical weapons waste. A safe and verifiable method for the collection, destruction, and disposal of military weapons, especially those involving nuclear, biological and chemical weapons, does not currently exist. If, however, the world was to agree to execute an agreement for total disarmament it seems logical to assume that one would be forthcoming. In this regard, a decision might also be needed in relation to the peaceful uses of nuclear power such as nuclear power plants. It is possible that the production of renewable energy sources, such as biological grains, wind, solar power and others will eventually make nuclear energy too costly to go on being used. If so, then the convention may decide to destroy and dispose of all nuclear materials in existence, whether intended for peaceful or military use.

It is, on the other hand, the disbandment and destruction of the existing conventional weaponry that may provide the greatest problems. It is difficult to imagine countries, such as North Korea disbanding their conventional military capability. It is just as hard to imagine countries such as the United States, the Russian Federation, China, and Great Britain disbanding their conventional military structure. The problem stems from the centuries-long competition that has existed under the current system of nationalism. The ingrained fear of the various nations will be very difficult to overcome in attempting to initiate an agreement for total disarmament.

It is not just fear, however, that would prove a difficulty, but also the pride that nations take in the status that efficient military institutions carry with them. No nation today is truly capable of withstanding a determined attack by the United States, even if Russia has sufficient nuclear power to make such an attack inadvisable; however, at the same time, very few nations do not maintain a military organization far beyond the reasonable budgetary restraints. In tackling this problem, the convention must consider two main solutions to the problem. First, whatever procedure is used to obtain a total disarmament agreement the various nations, and their citizens, must clearly understand that total disarmament is the only real security against external attack (a world union would eliminate any possibility of external attack by definition) and uncontrolled internal insurrection. Second, as proof of this statement it should be emphasized that in the two hundred plus years that the US has been in existence there has been only one occasion when one, or more, states have invaded the territory of another state, or states. This occasion was the civil war and by definition was not an external invasion but rather an internal insurrection. By ratifying the US Constitution the thirteen states agreed to disband their existing military organizations in favor of a solitary military organization under the control of the general government.

The military organization controlled by the general government would also have the power to intervene in cases of civil unrest if they should reach a level that was beyond the ability of the nation affected to quell. This power, however, would be contingent upon the general government receiving a request for aid from the affected nation, or the threat of an imminent collapse of that nation's government. In the latter case the general government would be authorized to use whatever force was necessary to quell the violence, but would also have the responsibility for providing a forum for the settlement of the dispute that led to the civil unrest. It must also be realized that each nation will be allowed to maintain whatever conventionally equipped force is necessary to internally enforce its own laws, as well as, to police criminal activities. In some cases it will be difficult in the extreme to determine the amount of conventional force that will be needed to execute these functions. It is assumed that in most cases the national police force will be equipped and operate in the same manner as they do today. It is only in nations where the military organization also doubles as the policing power that problems will arise.

The second expectation is that a judiciary be formed that is capable of acting as a final arbitrator of any disputes that might arise between member nations, member nations and the general government, the citizens of one member nation with the citizens of another member nation, or between a non-member nation, or its citizens, and a member nation, or its citizens. This is exactly the function that is served by the US Supreme Court, and the lower federal courts that are part of the US judicial system. Using the US system as a guide the general government would have a Supreme Court that would have the power to issue final verdicts in all cases under its jurisdiction. In some cases the Supreme Court would have original jurisdiction, that is, could hear the case without having to have it heard in a lower court. In the majority of cases, however, the Supreme Court would only have appellate jurisdiction, that is, it could only review cases that had been heard and upon which a verdict had been rendered by a lower court. The lower courts from which the Supreme Court could hear appeals would consist of the lower world government courts, such as the union's district courts and the union's court of appeals as in the United States; as well as the highest court of each nation. The Supreme Court would be the final arbitrator of the constitutionality of any law passed within the union whether passed by the general government or one of the member nations. This would include the provisions of any national constitution that might exist. It would not be the job of the convention to decide on the various levels of lower courts that would exist, or to make a decision concerning the number of these courts, or their locations. This type of planning would be the job of the first congress assembled after the ratification of the constitution. The federal district courts, in the case of the US system, are under normal circumstances the court of first review in regard to the citizens. As such it is necessary that they be located in a manner that makes it convenient for the citizens to use them. The federal appeals courts are just what their name suggests, that is, they do not have original jurisdiction but are only authorized to review cases that have been heard by a lower court, in the US system normally a federal district court. In the US, these courts are in essence regional courts and are placed to make them convenient for access from the region they serve. The Supreme Court, of course, would be located at the site designated as the capitol of the union. If non-members also existed it would be necessary to make provisions for the general government to cooperate in the establishment of an international court to settle any disputes that arose between the general government and the non-member nations.

The third expectation is one that needs little elaboration. Any government, to be effective, must have the power to pass necessary laws, edicts, and regulations to conduct the business expected of it, and the power to enforce those laws once duly passed. If the US example is followed, the legislative branch would have the sole responsibility for passing the laws, while the executive branch would have the sole responsibility of enforcing the laws, and the judiciary would have the sole duty of ruling upon the constitutionality of any given law.

The fourth expectation in the modern world is currently being met by granting the general government the power of taxation. If the US is used as a guide some taxation power will rest solely with the federal government (in this case the power to tax imports and exports). In the case of the world government this would be limited to certain taxes, such as luxury taxes, sin taxes, etc. Most of the taxing power would be concurrent with the same power in the national governments, such as income taxes, fuel taxes, license fees, etc. In one case the tax would be reserve solely for use by the national governments and whatever lower levels of government that existed within them, i.e., property taxes. It is suggested that the opportunity be taken to establish, through the constitution, an initial flat-rate income tax, not subject to deductions, that would periodically be subject to adjustment as to the rate of taxation only by the general legislature. However raised the income must be capable of maintaining the general government in its day-to-day operations, subject to the audit of its expenditures by the public.

The fifth expectation is one found in every successful government organization and in democratic systems in particular. This is the voluntary obedience to the laws of the vast majority of the citizens. Force should only be necessary to compel obedience from those who consciously decide to ignore or evade the duly passed laws. In general this would include all those who consciously engage in criminal activities as well as those who are normally law abiding citizens but who choose to ignore or disobey specific laws, such as traffic laws. I do not think that anyone can argue that the government that is most capable of long duration, and successful operation, will be the one that can maintain the voluntary obedience of its citizens. It can be presented as almost a tautology that the voluntary obedience of the citizens is given to the government perceived as the most representative of their interests and welfare. This expectation is most likely to be found in the citizens that feel that they have a real voice in who rules them, and the method by which they will be ruled. Included within this perception is the real possibility of being able to peacefully replace any who fail to meet the expectations of the citizens while in public service. These expectations are normally obtained to the highest degree, under modern conditions, when the government is formed on the basis of representative democracy. Obedience, however, can be either active or passive. Active obedience requires that the individual make a rational choice to obey each specific law after careful consideration of what the law requires of him. Passive obedience is of course obedience that is given out of fear of punishment or loss of status without consideration of the costs. It can only be hoped that any world government created will generate active obedience to its laws.

Once debate has been concluded concerning the powers that are to be delegated to the general government, denied to the nations, or that are to be held concurrently by both the general government and the member nations the convention will be faced with drafting a proposed constitution. It has been suggested throughout that the process of actually drafting the constitution would be most easily accomplished by using the US Constitution as a guide. The use of this guide could be stipulated at the time that the constitutional convention is initiated. It is likely that a guide of some type will be used by the convention even if one is not stipulated in their instructions. The reasons that have been set forth earlier will again be summarized here. First, and by far the most important, is that a constitution represents a written record of the intentions and desires of the delegates who drafted it. It also gives a solid basis to any interpretation of those intentions or desires, and lastly, it gives a solid basis for determining whether or not any specific law is in conflict with the constitution (the intentions and desires of the people). In the modern world it is inconceivable that a world government could be formed and successfully maintained without a written constitution. A liberal democracy is based upon the primal tenet that all power resides in the people. The only way that the people can safely delegate their power is in writing. It is only in this way that the people can satisfy themselves that those who exercise this power will remain under their control while in office. It is also the only way to insure that the people reserve the power to peacefully remove from office any person that they feel does not truly represent their interests and welfare. Second, the US Constitution represents the most durable and successful written constitution based on liberal democracy now in existence. Third, The US Constitution has shown itself to be a very flexible document capable of coping with changing conditions over a period exceeding two hundred years.

It will be assumed that the convention has been instructed to use the US Constitution as a guide in drafting a constitution for the proposed world government. This being the case it is possible to outline some of the general problems that will face the convention and need to be subjects of debate. The Federalist Papers set forth for us to read a group of general problems that faced the constitutional convention drafting the US Constitution. With a little adaptation it will become apparent that a constitutional convention called today would face the same problems. The first problem is explicitly set forth by Alexander Hamilton in the first of the papers, as follows: "The plan offered to our deliberations affects too many particular interests, innovates upon too many local institutions, not to invoke in its discussion a variety of objects foreign to its merits, and of views, passions and prejudices little favorable to the discovery of truth."[1] He later continues: "Among the most formidable of the obstacles which the new constitution will have to encounter may readily be distinguished the obvious interest of a certain class of men in every state to resist all changes which may hazard a diminution of the power, emolument, and consequences of the offices they hold under the state establishments; and the perceived ambition of another class of men, who will either hope to aggrandize themselves with fairer prospects of elevation from the subdivision of the empire into several partial confederacies than from the union under one government."[2] Although Hamilton intended this passage to apply to the process of ratifying the constitution, it applies equally well to the pressures that are likely to be felt by the delegates to the convention.

There can be no doubt that those who are delegates to the convention, or those whom they represent, may be in one or the other of these two classes of individuals. There also can be no doubt that the delegates, or those who instruct

---

1 *Great Books of the Western World.*, Robert Maynard Hutchins, Editor In Chief, Encyclopaedia, Inc., *The Federalist* Page 29

2 Ibid.

them, will be strongly attached to certain local interests, or local institutions, especially those concerning traditional cultural issues. It is hoped that this problem will be recognized as unavoidable and that it will be accepted for what it is limiting the time spent on debating the issues affected by it. For example, the president of the United States would no longer be recognized as the leader of an independent nation, but rather as the leader of one nation among many that maintain an equal status in the proposed union. Any debate that focused on increasing the importance of the president of the United States within the union should be recognized and accepted as an argument from interest. It will, of course, be an interest of both the people of the US and the then sitting president, as it will represent a significant decrease in the importance of both the country and the position of president. It is hoped that the citizens, and rulers, of any specific nation will be able to set aside the patriotism that supports the current system of nationalism and replace it with a genuine concern for the welfare of all people.

There were also several more practical issues that were pointed out in the Federalist Papers that are still relevant today. Some have been mentioned in earlier chapters but it is hoped that a review of them will be tolerable. First, it will be argued that the size of the world, coupled with the size of its population, will make it impossible for the government to operate efficiently. This argument has already been raised in relation to recent calls to reform the United Nations Charter. The arguments set forth in the Federalist Papers in 1789 were based upon questions of logistics. It was feared that it would take too long for the representatives, let alone the news of the actions taken by the government, to travel from their homes to the capitol. In short, the fear was that the representatives would not be able to maintain themselves away from home for the period of time needed to operate a government efficiently; and would also not be able to keep themselves sufficiently aware of their constituents needs. The answer given in the Federalist Papers are not relevant to the conditions that exist today, that is, the pointing out of historical governments that had operated efficiently in the past. Today the argument would be simply that the level of technology now available in the areas of transportation and communication would make such arguments obsolete. There does not appear to be any significant reason why a world government could not be both efficient and effective. Indeed, it may be fair to say that the smallness of the world in relation to the travel capabilities coupled with the growing interdependence of all people's demands that a unified government be established. In addition, since the end of the so-called "cold war" the existing nations have shown a willingness to consider systems of organization other than the current system of nationalism. At this time there are no ideological barriers to prevent the rational discussion of such a change. We may in fact never be in a better position to discuss a world government than in the conditions that currently exist. Second, it is likely that at least some discussion will arise concerning the need for a single unified world government versus a number of regional confederacies. The European Union represents an example of the type of organization that might appeal to people of this persuasion. A system of such unions could be envisioned covering the Asian Rim nations, the Pacific Island nations, North and South America, and Africa. Other combinations of unions of various nations could also be envisioned without much difficulty. The problem, however, with a number of confederacies even if they are established as sovereign governments is that it only reduces the number of "nations" that compose the system of nationalism. If there were only five unions, for example, there would still be a divergence of interests and concerns between them and they would exhibit the same reluctance to deal with problems such as environmental pollution. In the discussion of this issue by the Federalist Papers, the following points were brought forward and remain relevant today. It was pointed out that the first concern of a wise and free people was the providing for their own safety. This safety was seen as the best possible deterrent to external invasion by another nation and protection from insurrection within the society. This is still the first concern of all people, that is, they desire to live their lives free from danger of external invasion or danger from a violent internal insurrection. Both the Articles of Confederation and the United Nations Charter set forth as their primary goal the security of the people they represent. Neither was or has been capable of providing that security. Current events especially the invasion of Iraq clearly show that fears concerning external invasion are still real; as well as, the fear of ongoing violent civil wars most clearly represented by the so-called war on terrorism. It is obvious that the first goal of a world government, or a number of regional confederacies, would be to provide security from these two catastrophes. The arguments presented by the Federalist Papers were two fold, that is, first, that the cost and efficiency of providing five or six, or even two, military organizations capable of providing security of this type would be more than providing just one. Second, that history teaches us that the more nations there are in existence that more just and unjust causes there are for war to break out. The recent attack on the United States clearly points out that even the most powerful nations on earth are not immune from external invasion. History also confirms, through the experience of the United Nations, that when war is engaged it is most effectively prosecuted by having command in the hands of one leader as concerns strategy and day-to-day operations. Lastly, when there exist two hundred independently sovereign nations, or even five or six sovereign confederacies, business between the confederacies must be conducted on the basis of treaty or other contractual documents. Each of these documents represents the potential source of disagreement between the parties either just or unjust.

As the Federalist Papers point out, history provides us with no small number of wars that were waged both on just and unjust causes. In addition, although this argument was not available for use in the Federalist Papers, the history of the United States points out what might reasonably be expected with the establishment of a world government. In the history of the United States, there has not been one occasion in which one member state has justly or unjustly invaded the territory of another state. During this history, the fear of external invasion between the various states has been non-existent. It is likely that the same would be true of the member nations composing an effective world government. This same history also shows that there has been only one internal insurrection that was aimed at destroying the union. The civil war fought in the US however proves the validity of the argument that military engagements are better conducted by one government than by many as both combatants in this civil war operated under this assumption. All other internal disturbances within the US society have been demonstrations aimed at bringing public attention to the resolution of practical problems rather than the overturning of the system of government. It is likely that the establishment of a unified world government would provide the type of forum needed to effectively end the wars that are currently being waged in Afghanistan, Iraq, the Sudan and others. The United Nations has mandated a peace-keeping force to settle the civil war in Afghanistan and the Sudan, as well as committing itself to action in Eastern Europe; however, it has been powerless to intervene in the war being waged by the Chechnya rebels against the Russian Federation. The Russian Federation is a permanent member of the Security Council and is thereby empowered to veto any such mandate requested by the General Assembly. The invasion of Iraq by the US, for the same reason, is another clear example of the helpless position of the United Nations under its current charter to provide the type of security desired by the people of the world. In the latter two cases intervention has been limited to the application of world opinion which has been largely ineffective. Under a world government as envisioned herein the power to intervene would be available at the request of either the nation involved or the insurgency involved.

In the current environment assuming each nation was only allowed to maintain an internal policing organization the current military budget of the United States alone would be adequate to fund the general government's military institution. This assumes that each nation would reduce its policing organization to whatever level was needed to enforce its own laws and to prevent criminal behavior. As stated earlier it is assumed that these policing organizations would closely resemble those now found in most European nations and Japan. It also assumes that the type of security that is being discussed could be provided by the general government under these conditions with a conventionally equipped military of no great size. It is likely that the general government would face military challenges no greater than those represented by internal violent disturbances similar to those that have occasionally appeared in the United States. That is to say, the labor disputes of the twenties and thirties, the anti-war demonstrations of the 1970s and the civil rights riots of the late 70s and early 1980s. The various national policing organizations however might be taxed beyond their abilities if they were faced with internal insurrections such as those now found in Palestine, Afghanistan, Iraq and other areas. Currently these insurrections are collectively designated as terrorism losing sight of their existence as insurgencies. It may also be true that a conventional police force would not be able to handle the violence found in organized criminal activities such as those represented by drug cartels. It is expected however that the establishment of a world government will provide a peaceful judicial forum for the resolution of the type of issues that currently promote internal insurrection and violent organized criminal activity. It is also possible that a coordinated plan executed on a worldwide basis would soon eradicate the conditions that support the drug cartels and other organized criminal activities either by legalizing the use of controlled substances or by more stringent policing action. It must be remembered that, should violence within any individual nation or group of nations exceed the ability of that nation or nations to cope, they would have the right to request aid from the general government to quell the violence.

Lastly, the question was raised in the Federalist Papers over the general government's power to regulate international and interstate trade. In our situation of course assuming a unified world government there would be no such thing as international trade. If, however, a significant number of nations decided not to join the union and the union could be successful without them then some arrangements would have to be made for the conduct of commercial relations with the non-members. Because of the vast difference in commercial bargaining power this, in fact, might present a major problem for those nations who chose to stay outside the union. In the area of inter-nation trade the example of the European Union would point to the conclusion that a unified regulatory agency is not only desirable but a necessity. Currently international trade is subject only to the restrictions that are placed on it by means of treaties or other written contracts and a very loosely enforced international law. The recent growth of the global market, which is bringing the world's nations rapidly to the point of interdependence, has shown that a great deal of cooperation is needed. For example, very recently the United States ran into a serious economic problem involving the financing of the nation's homes. In response the Federal Reserve System put billions of dollars into circulation to shore up the lending institutions allowing them to loosen credit somewhat. What is even more relevant is that the Federal Reserve System was able to convince the largest banks in the international market to do the same in regard to their national partners. This, and other events, show that the need for unified regulation of financial, industrial, commercial, and monetary practices is not too far in the future regardless of the action taken in regard to a world government.

The above should be enough to make it obvious that the same problems which existed in 1789 also exist in the political environment of 2009. A convention called to draft a constitution for world government, therefore, would be faced with providing such a constitution with provisions designed to resolve or at least to provide means whereby these problems could be resolved. There are several ways in which the drafting of this constitution could be approached but none seem more effective than using the US Constitution as a guide.

The most convenient, and possibly the easiest to obtain agreement upon, would be to call for a convention to reform the United Nations Charter. This was in fact the method chosen by those in the early United States that wanted to replace the Articles of Confederation. The United Nations Charter was written at the end of World War II and represents the environment that existed at the very beginning of the cold war. The cold war quickly became a battle between two competing economies. The cold war of course was described largely as being between two diametrically opposed political systems, but it was mainly driven by political interests. The position taken by the Soviet Union was based upon the goals of socialism as set forth by Karl Marx and adapted by Vladimir Lenin, and it assumed the eventuality of the natural demise of capitalism and the establishment of a worldwide communal order. The US adopted the ideological position that the Soviet philosophy was opposed to the principles of liberal democracy and that it should be fought everywhere that it appeared. This latter philosophy was captured in the unofficial doctrine of containment adopted by the United States. Over five or six decades, the two sides attempted to promote their positions by supporting governments favorable to their philosophy either militarily or economically. Each side attempted to surround itself with a bloc of nations that would support it in the face of world opinion, particularly as world opinion was displayed in the General Assembly of the United Nations. The General Assembly however was of relative insignificance except as a barometer of world opinion. The real policy control within the United Nations had been settled in the Security Council. The council had five permanent members, all of which were capable of vetoing any action taken by the U.N. general assembly. The five members were the most powerful members of both sides of the ideological battle, that is, the United States, Great Britain, and France on the one side, and the Soviet Union and the Republic of China on the other. Under the conditions of the developing cold war the structure of the United Nations guaranteed its ineffectiveness from the very beginning. The history of the first forty years of operation under these conditions only confirms these hypotheses.

The situation however has changed over the last two decades. The cold war and the policies that went with it have come to an unexpected end with the demise of the Soviet system of government. The new Russian Federation has taken its place on the Security Council. China has become a member of the world community. The nations that once were courted by both sides in the cold war are now left to fend for themselves with aid coming from various nations, the European Union, or through the United Nations. The General Assembly as a result has become more important in shaping the national policies of the various nations through the effective use of world opinion. It remains however impotent in relationship to the veto power still residing in the permanent Security Council members. It is still true that the current structure of the United Nations puts it in exactly the same position as the Articles of Confederation, that is, the Articles were not effective in providing government for the confederacy and the U.N. Charter is not effective as a world government. The reformation of the United Nations does not for these reasons seem to be a wise choice in attempting to establish an effective world government.

The point being made is that conditions that exist today are really not that different from those that existed in 1789. Many individuals have recognized this fact but to date no serious attempts have been made to reform the United Nations Charter. In fact, very little has been extended to the public at large concerning the need for such a reform. Indeed, there has not to date even been an attempt to establish an international authority to arbitrate disputes of a political, cultural, or economic nature. This international forum if created separate from a world government would not be expected to arbitrate military disputes; and probably would not act as a court in the interpretation of treaties and contracts, but would act solely as a beginning point for the discussion and resolution of such problems as environmental pollution. Not even this small step has been able to come about under the current system of nationalism. The convention might begin its work by taking a look at the content of Federalist Papers number ten. This paper begins with the statement that the function of all government is to regulate faction. By faction is meant all the disputes that arise from whatever source because of differing positions taken by individual citizens or groups of citizens. These disputes can be of many different types, for example, they might be political, economic, social, or religious. The argument begins with the simple statement that no one should be the judge in his own case because of the prejudice found in such situations. Since it can be accepted that faction is a normal component of every society the best that can be hoped for is that faction will be controlled in such a manner that the underlying society is not destroyed. The core idea behind representative democracy is that each citizen should be allowed the opportunity to make their interests known; and that, through the use of compromise a solution will be provided that is satisfactory to all interests. In a representative democracy this process is one step removed from the people as a whole, that is, the debate and compromise is conducted by the representatives of the people rather the people themselves. The election of representatives is itself a compromise as everyone will not vote for the same representative in any given election. The compromise being that a set number of votes will be accepted as arbitrarily expressing the will of the people at large in regard to the representatives. Each representative will have constituents with differing interests and will attempt to have these interests heard. The legislative body as a whole will debate the various issues brought before it and through compromise will accept and pass into law those that can garner the requisite support. The benefit of the republican representative democracy based on a written constitution is that it allows the people to determine which powers will be granted or denied to the various levels of government with all others being retained by the people.

In conclusion it should be understood that a specific objection will certainly be raised to the use of the representative republican democracy format. This argument will point out the fact that all thirteen of the proposed members of the US union already had in operation that form of government. In addition, the people of the thirteen states had inherited over a century and one half of experience in operating as self-ruled people. The argument will then set in opposition to this state of affairs the fact that the existing nations contained a significant number that have not currently a democratic system and which are composed of people with no experience in self-rule. The argument will undoubtedly end in one of two ways. First, it could end with the conclusion that the difference in circumstances will lead directly to the failure of any attempt to establish a democratic world government. Second, that the difference in circumstances will require that the laws passed by the general government should apply only to the member nations in their corporate capacity and not to the citizens of these nations. The premise of the first conclusion cannot be challenged directly as it is true that a significant number of nations, and peoples, are not currently living under a democratic government and that they have little or no experience of self-rule. It is also true that even less have had experience with a representative republican democracy based upon a written constitution. The most that can be offered in response to this conclusion is that since the end of World War II a relatively large number of nations and people have adopted democratic governments without the prior experience of either democracy or self-rule, for example, Japan and India. A very large proportion of these nations have been successful in operating and maintaining this form of government regardless of the lack of experience. It must also be remarked along these lines that short of disbanding totally the existing system of nationalism a republican form of government is the only one with any chance of success. In response to the second conclusion it must be restated that the core tenet of representative republican democracy and liberal democracy in general, is that all power initially resides with the people at large. The people cannot be the source of any power that does not apply to them directly. Under liberal democracy the people are under the duty to make a rational choice as to whether or not the laws passed by the government are to be obeyed or not. One of the main weaknesses of the Articles and the U.N. Charter is the fact that in both cases the laws, or mandates in the case of the U.N., applied only to the states or member nations in their corporate capacity. This allowed the situation where the state or nation could decide whether or not to obey the law or mandate regardless of the wishes of the people.

If the convention were to create a constitution instituting a representative republican democracy what power would the nations be required to give up as members of the new government. Some of the most important are as follows. First, the several nations will be required to give up the right to create and maintain separate military organizations. The several nations as outlined above would be allowed to maintain an internal police force. Second, the several nations will be required to give up or at least share their power of taxation in regard to their citizens. Third, the several nations will be required to give up their sole control of trade between themselves and other nations. They will still be in sole control of the trade that is conducted exclusively within their national borders. They would give up the sole power to resolve any disputes over trade that might arise between them, i.e., they would have to accept the general government as the final arbitrator of trade disputes. Fourth, the several nations would have to give up their power to create and value independent monetary systems, independent systems of weights and measures, independent systems of taxation on imports and exports, and independent regulation of common areas, such as the open seas, outer space, and cyberspace. Fifth, the several nations will be required to give up the exclusive sovereignty of their national laws, that is to say, they will have to accept the general laws, edicts, and regulations passed by the general government as the supreme laws of the union. Lastly, the several nations would be required to give up their sole control over pollution, the use of natural resources, and the disposal of toxic wastes. They would however still be required to execute and enforce the laws and regulations passed in these areas by the general government. Much more will be said concerning all of these points as we proceed.

Chapter 5. A Sketch for a World Constitution

The reasons or arguments relating to the support of the timing, the creation, and the institution of an effective world government have been set forth in the preceding chapter. Other arguments surely exist that could more clearly and cogently support this proposal, and the arguments actually used no doubt could have been presented with more effect. It is also certain that many issues, objections, and arguments will be raised both for and against world government, and the constitution created to support it that have not been taken into consideration in the foregoing chapter. Accepting all this as true this chapter will now begin the detailed look at the Federalist Papers as they attempt to explain to the public of 1789 what was contained and intended to be contained in the proposed US Constitution.

Although we have quoted a passage from Federalist Papers No. 1 for another purpose, I believe it to be worthwhile to begin our discussion by quoting this number in full. As stated earlier, No. 1 is believed to have been written by Alexander Hamilton. It sets the mood for all the discussion that follows in the succeeding numbers of the papers and is imperative to an understanding of the arguments used in favor of ratifying the US Constitution.

> After an unequivocal experience of the inefficiency of the existing federal government, you are called upon to deliberate on a new constitution for the United States of America. The subject speaks its own importance; comprehending in its consequences nothing less than the existence of the UNION, the safety and welfare of the parts of which it is composed, the fate of an empire in many respects the most interesting in the world. It has been frequently remarked that it seems to have been reserved to the people of this country, by their conduct and example, to decide the impor-

tant question, whether societies of men are capable or not of establishing good government from reflection and choice, or whether they are forever destined to depend for their political constitutions on accident and force. If there be any truth in the remark, the crisis at which we are arrived may with propriety be regarded as the era in which that decision is to be made; and a wrong election of the part we shall act may, in this view, deserve to be considered as the general misfortune of mankind.

This idea will add inducements of philanthropy to those of patriotism, to heighten the solicitude which all considerate and good men must feel for the event. Happy will it be if our choice should be directed by a judicious estimate of our true interests, unperplexed and unbiased by considerations not connected with the public good. But this is a thing more ardently to be wished than seriously to be expected. The plan offered to our deliberations affects too many particular interests, innovates upon too many local institutions, not to invoke in its discussions a variety of objects foreign to its merits, and of views, passions, and prejudices little favorable to the discovery of truth.

Among the most formidable of the obstacles which the new constitution will have to encounter may readily be distinguished the obvious interests of a certain class of men in every state to resist all changes which may hazard a diminution of power, emolument, and consequences of the offices they hold under the state establishments; and the perverted ambition of another class of men, who will either hope to aggrandize themselves by the confusions of their country, or will flatter themselves with fairer prospects of elevation from the subdivision of the empire into several partial confederacies than from the union under one government.

It is not, however, my design to dwell upon observations of this nature. I am well aware that it would be disingenuous to resolve indiscriminately the opposition of any set of men (merely because their situations might subject them to suspicion) into interested or ambitious views. Candor will oblige us to admit that even such men may be actuated by upright intentions; and it cannot be doubted that much of the opposition which has made its appearance, or may hereafter make its appearance, will spring from sources, blameless at least, if not respectable-the honest errors of minds led astray by preconceived jealousies and fears. So numerous indeed and so powerful are the causes which serve to give a false bias to the judgment, that we, upon many occasions, see wise and good men on the wrong, as well as the on the right side of questions of the first magnitude to society. This circumstance, if duly attended to, would furnish a lesson of moderation to those who ever so much persuaded of their being right in any controversy. And a further caution, in this respect, might be drawn from the reflection that we are not always sure that those who advocate the truth are influenced by purer principles than their antagonists. Ambition, avarice, personal animosity, party opposition, and many other motives not more laudable than those, are apt to operate as well upon those who support as those who oppose the right side of a question. Were not even those inducements to moderation, nothing could be more ill-judged than that intolerant spirit which has, at all times, characterized political parties. For in politics, as in religion, it is equally absurd to aim at making proselytes by fire and sword. Heresies in either can rarely be cured by persecution.

And yet, however, just these sentiments will be allowed to be, we have already sufficient indications that it will happen in this as in all former cases of great national discussion. A torrent of angry and malignant passions will be let loose. To judge from the conduct of the opposite parties, we shall be led to conclude that they will actually hope to evince the justness of their opinions and to increase the number of their converts by the loudness of their declamations and the bitterness of their invectives. An enlightened zeal for the energy and efficiency of government will be stigmatized as the offspring of a temper fond of despotic power and hostile to the principles of liberty. An overscrupulous jealousy of danger to the rights of the people, which is more commonly the fault of the head than of the heart, will be represented as mere pretence and artifice, the stale bait for popularity at the expense of the public good. It will not be forgotten, on the on the one hand, that jealousy is the usual concomitant of love, and that the noble enthusiasm of liberty is apt to be infected with a spirit of narrow and illiberal distrust. On the other hand, it will be equally forgotten that the vigor of government is essential to the security of liberty; that, in the contemplation of a sound and well-informed judgment, their interest can never be separated; and that a dangerous ambition more often lies behind the specious mask of zeal for the rights of the people than under the forbidding appearance of zeal for the firmness and efficiency of government. History will teach us that the former has been found a much more certain road to the introduction of despotism than the latter, and that those men who have overturned the liberties of republics, the greatest number have begun their careers paying an obsequious court to the people, commencing demagogues, and ending tyrants.

In the course of the preceding observations, I have had an eye, my fellow citizens, to putting you upon your guard against attempts, from whatever quarter, to influence your decision, in a matter of the utmost moment to your welfare, by any impressions other than those which may result from the evidence of truth. You will, no doubt, at the same time, have collected from the general scope of them that they precede from a source not unfriendly to the new constitution. Yes, my country-men, I own to you that after having given it an attentive consideration, I am clearly of the opinion it is your interest to adopt it. I am convinced that this is the safest course for your liberty, your dignity, and your happiness. I affect not reserves which I do not feel. I will not amuse you with an appearance of deliberation when I have decided. I frankly acknowledge to you my convictions, and I will freely lay before you the reasons on which they are founded. The consciousness of good intentions distains ambiguity. I shall not, however, multiply professions on this head. My motives must remain in the depository of my own breast. My arguments will be open to all, and may be judged by all. They shall at least be offered in a spirit which will not disgrace the cause of truth.

I propose, in a series of papers, to discuss the following interesting particulars: the utility of the UNION to your political prosperity-the insufficiency of the present confederation to preserve the union-the necessity of a government at least equally energetic with the one proposed; to the attainment of this object-the conformity of the proposed constitution to the true principles of republican government-its analogy to your own state constitutions-and lastly *the additional security which its adoption will afford to the preservation of that species of government, to liberty, and to property.*

In the progress of this discussion I shall endeavor to give a satisfactory answer to all the objections which shall have made their appearance, that may seem to have any claim to your attention.

It may perhaps be thought superfluous to offer arguments to prove the utility of the UNION, a point, no doubt, deeply engraved on the hearts of the great body of the people in every state, and one which, it may be imagined, has no adversaries. But the fact is, that we already hear it whispered in the private circles of those who oppose the new constitution, that the thirteen states are too great an extent for any general system, and that we must of necessity resort to separate confederacies of distinct portions of the whole. This doctrine will, in all probability, be gradually proposed, till it has votaries enough to countenance an open avowal of it. For nothing can be more evident, to those who are able to take an enlarged view of the subject, than the alternative of an adoption of the new constitution or a dismemberment of the union. It will therefore be of use to begin by examining the advantages of that union, the certain evils, and the probable dangers, to which every state will be exposed from its dissolution. This shall accordingly constitute the subject of my next address. Publius[1]

It is assumed that the reader will substitute the appropriate words to apply this address to our current environment and will overlook the prejudices of the time including gender value statements.

Next we can sketch out a proposed constitution for a world government. This, of course, is in no way intended to represent what might result from a constitutional convention but merely to provide a basis for debate concerning the problems such a constitution might face.

THE CONSTITUTION OF THE UNITED NATIONS OF EARTH

Preamble

We the people of Earth, in order to form a desired union, to establish justice, insure domestic tranquility, provide common defense, promote the general welfare do establish this constitution for the United Nations of Earth.

Article One

Section 1. All legislative powers granted by this constitution shall reside in a congress of the United Nations of Earth, which will consist of a Senate and House of Representatives.

Section 2. The House of Representatives will be made up of members chosen every second year by the people of the several nations and the electors in each

1 Ibid.

nation will have the qualifications necessary for electors of the most numerous branch of the nation's legislature.

No person shall be a representative who has not attained the age of twenty-five, and who has not been a citizen of the nation that elects them for a period of seven years. The representative must be a resident citizen of the nation that elects them at the time of the election.

Representatives, will be apportioned among the several nations that are included as members of the union according to their respective populations as determined by a census to be conducted within three years from the adoption of this constitution. Such a census shall include every person who has attained the age of eighteen years. This census and the apportionments it determines will be conducted every ten years. The number of representatives for any nation shall not exceed twenty five, but each nation will have at least one representative.

When vacancies happen in the representatives from any nation, the executive authority of that nation will cause a new election to be held as soon as possible to fill the said vacancy.

The House of Representatives will choose their own officers, and has the sole power of impeachment.

Section 3.The Senate of the United Nations of Earth will consist of two senators from each nation, chosen by the legislature of that nation, for a period of six years, and each senator will have one vote.

Immediately after the first assembly has come into being they will be divided as equally as possible into three classes. The seats of the first class will be vacated at the end of two years, the second at the end of four years, and the third at the end of six years, so that one third of the Senate is elected every second year.

Vacancies as they occur will be filled by appointment by the executive officer of the nation where the vacancy occurs until the next senator is appointed by that nation's legislative branch.

No person will be a senator who has not attained the age of thirty years, and who has not been a citizen of the nation that elects them for nine years. The senator must be a resident citizen of the nation that elects them at the time of the election.

The Vice-President of the United Nations of Earth will be the presiding officer in the Senate, but shall have no vote, unless to break a tie vote. The Senate shall choose all its other officers, including a person to act as presiding officer in case of the disability of the Vice-President, or his serving as President of the United Nations of Earth.

The Senate shall have the sole power to try all cases of impeachment brought by the House of Representatives. The Chief Justice of the Supreme Court will preside in the case of impeachment being brought against the President of the United Nations of Earth. No person shall be convicted without the concurrence of two-thirds of the members present. Judgment in cases of impeachment will go no further than to disqualify the impeached person from holding any office within the United Nations of Earth. The convicted party, however, will still be held capable of civil or criminal action if a law has been violated.

Section 4. The times, places, and manner of holding elections for senators and representatives shall be established by the legislature of that nation, but congress may at any time fix the times, places, and manner of elections by law made or after such regulation, except as to the manner of choosing senators. The congress shall assemble every year beginning the first Monday of every January and sit in constant session until the last Friday of every November.

Section 5. Each branch of the legislature will judge of the elections, returns, and qualifications of its own members and a majority of each will constitute a quorum to do business; but a smaller number may adjourn from day to day. Each house shall have the power to compel attendance from its members in such manner, and under such penalties as each house sees fit. Each will determine the rules of its proceedings, punish its members for misconduct, and with concurrence of two-thirds of its members, expel a member.

Each house will keep a journal of its proceedings, including the vote of each member, or abstention by a member, on every issue that comes before it. The journal of each house will be published by the second Monday of every December and made available, at no cost, to anyone who requests a copy.

Neither house during the session of congress shall adjourn for more than three days without the consent of the other house. Neither house will be authorized to meet at any other place than that designated as the congress of the United Nations of Earth.

Section 6. The senators and representatives will receive a compensation for their services to be established by law and paid out of the treasury of the United Nations of Earth. They will be privileged from arrest during the session of congress, except for cases of felony and breach of the peace. This privilege will include travel to and from a session of congress. They will not be held liable for the content of any speech delivered while congress is in session.

No senator or representative will during the time for which they are elected be eligible for appointment to any civil office under the authority of the United Nations of Earth, which shall have been created, or the emoluments have been increased during such time; and no person holding any office under the United Nations of Earth shall be a member of either house during continuance in office.

Section 7. All bills for raising revenue shall originate in the House of Representatives; but the Senate may propose or concur with amendments as on other bills. Every bill that has passed the House of Representatives and the Senate before it becomes law must be signed by the President of the United Nations of Earth; if approved the President shall sign it, but if not the President will return it with objections, to the house where it originated. The house will then enter the objections into its journal and reconsider it. After reconsideration the bill may be repassed by a two-thirds concurrence. The bill will be sent to the other house where it will undergo the same reconsideration to objections and repassage. If approved by two-thirds of each house the bill will become law. If the bill is not returned in ten days, excluding Sundays and holidays, the bill will become law.

Every order, resolution, or vote to which concurrence of the Senate and House of Representatives is necessary (except adjournment) will be presented to the President of the United Nations of Earth, and before taking effect, will be approved by, or being vetoed by the President, shall be repassed by two-thirds of the House of Representatives and Senate according to the rules and limitations prescribed in the case of a bill.

> Section 8. The congress will have power to lay and collect taxes as determined by law, to pay the debts and provide for the common defense and general welfare of the United Nations of Earth, but all taxes imposed must be uniform throughout the union.

- To borrow money on the credit of the United Nations of Earth.
- To regulate commerce among the several nations.
- To establish and regulate the value of a unified monetary standard, and to establish a uniform standard of weights and measures.
- To provide laws against the counterfeiting of the securities or money of the United Nations of Earth, and to provide punishment for such counterfeiting.
- To establish a uniform postal service throughout the union.
- To promote the progress of science and the useful arts by securing for a limited time to authors and inventors the exclusive right to their respective writings and discoveries.
- To regulate the use and promote the uniformity of the cyberspace system (Internet) throughout the union, as well as all common areas, such as outer space, the open seas, Antarctica and the Arctic and to provide punishment for the misuse of cyberspace, outer space, or the open seas.
- To establish courts inferior to the Supreme Court of the United Nations of Earth.
- To declare war.
- To raise and support a military, but an appropriation of money to that use shall be for a term no longer than two years.
- To provide and maintain a navy and air force, and all Special Forces, or policing authorities deemed necessary, by law. No nation will be allowed to create or maintain a militia, navy, air force, or Special Forces unit with the exception of a national policing organization specifically for use within that nation's internal border.
- To exercise sole jurisdiction over the district assigned as the base of operation for the United Nations of Earth, such district not to exceed ten square miles, or the equivalent in kilometers, which ever measure is used. The con-

gress will exercise a like authority over any building, or installation, approved by the legislature of the nation in which it is found, for whatever needful purpose as approved by law. Such necessary additions to the United Nations of Earth are to be purchased from the nation involved at a fairly negotiated price.

• To make all laws necessary and proper for putting in force the foregoing powers, and all other powers vested by this constitution in the government of the United Nations of Earth, or any department or officer thereof.

Section 9. The congress is authorized to establish a uniform system of ingress and egress from all nations for the citizens of all nations as established by law. Any, and all passports, visas, or other travel documents required, if any, shall be uniform throughout the union.

The privilege of writ of habeas corpus shall not be suspended, even in cases of rebellion or where the public safety is in danger.

No bill of attainder or ex post facto law shall be passed.

No tax or duty shall be laid on articles exported from any nation, or that is imported by any nation, other than that necessary to enforce its inspection laws. No preference shall be given by any regulation of commerce or revenue to the ports of any one nation over those of another; nor will vessels bound to or from one nation be obligated to enter, clear, or pay duties in another.

No money will be drawn from the treasury except by appropriations made by law, and a regular statement and accounting of the receipts and expenditures of all public money will be published each year at the end of November and be made available to anyone who cares to inspect it at no cost.

Section 10. No nation will enter into any treaty, alliance, or confederation, coin money, emit bills of credit; or make anything but that which the United Nations of Earth, by law, authorizes as tender in payment of debts; pass any bill of attainder, ex post facto law, or law impairing the obligation of contracts. No nation will, without the consent of congress, lay any imposts or duties on imports or exports, except what is absolutely necessary for executing its inspection laws; and the net produce of all duties and imposts, laid by any nation on imports and exports, will be for the use of the treasury of the United Nations of Earth; and all such laws will be subject to revision and control of congress.

No nation will, with the consent of congress, lay any duty of tonnage, keep troops or ships of war in time of peace, enter into any agreement or compact with any other nation, or engage in war, unless actually invaded or in such imminent danger as will not admit of delay.

Article Two

Section 1The executive power will be invested in a President of the United Nations of Earth. The President shall hold office during the term of four years, and together with the Vice-President, chosen for the same term, be elected as follows: Each nation will appoint, in such manner as the legislative branch of each nation shall direct, a number of electors, equal to the whole number of senators and representatives to which that nation is entitled in congress, but no senator or representative, or person holding an office or trust or profit under the United Nations of Earth will be appointed elector.

The electors will meet in their respective nations and vote by ballot for two persons, of whom at least one shall not be a resident of the same nation as themselves. The names of the two persons elected by a majority vote of the electors of each nation will be drawn up in a list and delivered to the congress of the United Nations of Earth, directed to the President of the Senate. The President of the Senate, in the joint presence of the members of the Senate and House of Representatives will put the list up for election by the majority of all members of congress. Such election shall be conducted by electronic ballot, and continue until one person has obtained the majority of votes, one for President and one for Vice-President. If after the first ballot more than one person for each office has a majority of votes, or an equal number of votes, the congress shall take the top five candidates for each office and proceed to a second vote. Each nation's delegation to congress, both senators and representatives combined, will each have one vote.

Congress may by amendment to this constitution by two-thirds vote of both houses, designate a different form of electing the President and Vice-President, provided such amendment is approved by three-fourths of the legislative branches of the member nations.

Congress may determine the time of choosing electors and the day on which they will deliver their votes, which day and time will be uniform throughout the union.

No person will be qualified as President or Vice-President unless being of the age of thirty-five years.

In case of removal of the President from office, or of the Presidents death, resignation, or inability to discharge the duties of President, the Vice-President shall become acting President for the remainder of the term in office. Congress will have the power, by law, to designate which officer, or officers, shall become President if both the President and the Vice-President are removed from office, die, or become unable to discharge the duties of the office of President.

The President and Vice-President will be compensated in a manner designated by law which compensation will neither decrease or increase during the term in office. During the term in office the President and Vice-President shall receive no other compensation, or emolument from the United Nations of Earth, or from any member nation, or any of their citizens. The compensation in place at the end of the last term served by the President and Vice-President shall constitute a lifetime pension.

Congress may designate an oath of office to be sworn to by the President and Vice-President elect, before taking office. The oath of office will not be used as a test of religious belief or any other test except adherence to this constitution and its contents.

Section 2. The President will be commander in chief of the military forces of the United Nations of Earth. The President may require, in writing, of the principle officers in each of the executive departments, upon any subject relating to the duties of the respective offices, and will have the power to grant reprieves and pardons for offenses against the United Nations of Earth, except in cases of impeachment.

The President will have the power, by and with the advice and consent of the Senate, to make treaties, provided two-thirds of the Senators present concur; and the President will nominate, and, by and with the consent of the Senate, appoint public ministers and consuls, justices of the Supreme Court, and all other officers of the United Nations of Earth whose appointments are not herein otherwise provided for, and which will be established by law, but congress may by law rest the appointment of such inferior officers, as they think proper, in the President alone, in the courts of law, or in the heads of departments.

The President will have the power to fill vacancies during the recess of the Senate, by granting commissions, which will expire at the end of their next session.

Section 3. The President each year on the 2nd Friday of January will give to the congress information concerning the state of the union, and recommend to their consideration such measures as the President judges expedient; he may, on extra-ordinary occasions, convene both houses of congress, or either of them, and in case of disagreement between them in this respect to the time of adjournment, he may adjourn them to such time as he thinks proper. The President will be empowered to faithfully see that the laws of the union are executed and will commission all officers of the United Nations of Earth.

Section 4. The President, Vice-President, and all civil officers of the United Nations of Earth will be removed from office on impeachment for and conviction of bribery, or other high crimes and misdemeanors.

Article Three

Section 1. The judicial power of the United Nations of Earth will be vested in one Supreme Court and in such inferior courts as the congress may from time to time ordain and establish. The judges, both for the Supreme Court, and the inferior courts, will hold office during good behavior, and will, at stated times, be compensated for their services, which compensation will not be diminished during their continuance in office.

Section 2. The judicial power will extend to all cases in law and equity, arising under this constitution, and the laws of the United Nations of Earth, affecting the powers of the United Nations of Earth, or controversies between any two or more nations, or between the citizens of one nation against another nation, or between the citizens of two or more nations.

In all cases in which a member nation or the United Nations of Earth is a party, the Supreme Court shall have original jurisdiction. In all other cases mentioned the Supreme Court will have appellate jurisdiction, both as to law and fact, with such exceptions and under such regulations as the congress shall make.

The trial of all crimes, except cases of impeachment, shall be by jury; and such trial shall be held in the nation where the said crime shall have been committed; but when not committed in any nation, the trial will be at such place or places as the congress may by law have directed.

Section 3 Treason against the United Nations of Earth will consist of levying war against any member nation, or the commission of acts of internal insurrection, as defined by law, against any member nation, or the United Nations of Earth. No person shall be convicted of treason unless granted all due process of law at a public trial by jury.

The congress will have the power to declare punishment for treason, but no attainder of treason shall be attributed to any other person beyond the person attainted.

Article Four

Section 1. Full faith and credit will be given in each nation to the public acts, records, and judicial proceedings of every other nation. Congress may by general laws prescribe the manner in which such acts, records, and proceedings will be proved, and the effect thereof.

Section 2. The citizens of each nation will be entitled to all the privileges and immunities of the citizens in the several nations.

A person charged in any nation with treason, felony, or other crime, who will flee from justice, and be found in another nation, shall, on demand of the executive officer of the nation from where they fled, be delivered up, to be removed to the nation having jurisdiction of the crime.

No person may be held to service or labor in any nation, or in the United Nations of Earth, against their consent, or by obligation of contract.

Section 3. New nations, or nations who chose not to be members of the union at the date this union commences, may be admitted to the union by a two-thirds vote of both houses of congress. No nation may be formed or erected within the boundaries of any nation established and becoming a member of this union or formed by the junction of two or more nations or parts of nations, when members of the union without the consent of the legislatures of the nations concerned as well as the congress of the United Nations of Earth.

The congress will have the power to dispose of and make all needful rules and regulations respecting the property belonging to the United Nations of Earth; and nothing in this constitution will be so construed as to prejudice any claims of the United Nations of Earth or of any particular nation.

Section 4. The United Nations of Earth shall guarantee to every nation in this union the free institution and operation of the government of its choice and shall protect each of them from invasion, and on application of the legislature, or executive department of the nation affected against domestic violence.

Congress may also determine by law what conditions of domestic violence or rebellion in any nation lacking application for aid from the nation involved, empowers the United Nations of Earth to intervene civilly or militarily.

Article Five

The congress whenever two-thirds of both houses will deem it necessary, will propose amendments to this constitution, or, on the application of the legislatures of two-thirds of the several member nations, shall call a convention for proposing amendments, which in either case, will be valid to all intents and purposes, as part of this constitution, when ratified by the legislatures of three-fourths of the nations then members of the union, or by conventions in three-fourths thereof, as the one or the other mode of ratification may be proposed by the congress; provided that no amendment deprives any nation of its equal suffrage in the Senate, or representation in the House of Representatives.

Article Six

This constitution and the laws of the United Nations of Earth which will be made in pursuance thereof, and all treaties made under the authority of the United Nations of Earth, will be the supreme law of the union; and the judges in every nation will be bound thereby, anything in the constitution, laws, or religious edits of any nation to the contrary notwithstanding.

Article Seven

The ratification of the conventions of three-fourths of the nations originally seeking admission to the union will be sufficient for the establishment of this constitution between the nations so ratifying the same.

Article Eight

Congress will make no law respecting the establishment of religion, or prohibiting the free exercise thereof; or abridging the freedom of speech, or of the press, or the right of the people peacefully to assemble and to petition the government for a redress of grievances.

Article Nine

The right of the people to be secure in their persons, houses, papers, and effects, against unreasonable searches and seizures, will not be violated, and no warrants will issue, but upon probable cause, supported by an oath or affirmation, and particularly describing the place to be searched, and the persons and things to be seized.

Article Ten

No person shall be held to answer for a capital, or otherwise infamous crime, unless on a presentment or indictment of a grand jury, nor will any person be subject to the same offense to be twice in jeopardy of life, limb; nor be compelled in any criminal case to be a witness against themselves, nor be deprived of life, liberty, or property, without due process of law; nor will private property be taken for public use, without just compensation.

Article Eleven

In all criminal prosecutions the accused will enjoy the right to a speedy and public trial, by an impartial jury of the nation and district wherein the crime has been committed, which district will have been previously ascertained by law, and to be informed of the nature and cause of the accusation; to be confronted with the witnesses against them; to have a compulsory process of obtaining witnesses in their favor, and to have the assistance of counsel for their defense, and if counsel cannot be afforded, the right to have counsel appointed for them free of obligation.

Article Twelve

Congress may, under conditions it determines by law, provide for trial by jury in civil cases.

Article Thirteen

Excessive bail will not be required, nor excessive fines imposed, nor cruel and unusual punishment inflicted in the case of accusation or conviction for any crime.

Article Fourteen

The enumeration in the constitution of certain rights shall not be construed to deny or disparage others retained by the people.

Article Fifteen

The powers not delegated to the United Nations of Earth by this constitution, nor prohibited by it to the member nations, are reserved to the nations respectfully or to the people.

Article Sixteen

The congress will be empowered to issue laws, ordinances, and regulations for the conservation and use of the member nations natural resources, and the natural resources found in all common areas, such as the open seas, uninhabited land masses, outer space and any others, as it from time to time sees fit; all such laws, ordinances, and regulations to be executed and enforced uniformly throughout the union.

The congress will be empowered to make laws, ordinances, and regulations concerning the producing, destruction, or disposal, of toxic, or noxious, or otherwise dangerous emissions resulting from the use of fossil fuels, or from any other source whatsoever, as it deems necessary, the implementation and enforcement of such laws, ordinances, and regulations to be uniform throughout the union.

Article Seventeen

The judicial power of the United Nations of Earth will not be construed to extend to any case in law or equity, commenced or prosecuted against one of the member nations citizens, or the citizens or subjects of any nation not a member of the union, however, congress may determine by law the manner in which such cases will be treated.

Article Eighteen

Neither slavery nor involuntary servitude, except as punishment for crime, where of the party will have been convicted will exist within the United Nations of Earth, or any place subject to its jurisdiction. Congress will have the power to enforce this article by appropriate legislation.

Article Nineteen

Section 1. All persons of every member nation are citizens of the United Nations of Earth and of the nation wherein they reside. No nation shall abridge the privileges or immunities of the citizens of the United Nations of Earth, nor shall any nation deprive any person of life, liberty, or property without due process of law; nor deny to any person the equal protection of the laws.

Section 2. Representatives shall be apportioned among the member nations according to the method designated in this constitution. The right to vote will be accorded every person who has attained the age eighteen years, without exception, in all elections affecting any office of the United Nations of Earth subject to election by ballot of the people. If the vote is denied to any person who attains the age of eighteen years, for any reason, in any nation for the legislative members, the executive members, or others subject to election by ballot of the people of the member nation, that nations representation in the House of Representatives will be reduced, with the sole exception that all nations be allowed at least one representative.

Section 3. No person duly convicted of treason will be allowed to be President, Vice-President, or hold any office civil or military, in either the United Nations of Earth, or any member nation respectfully. Congress may by two-thirds vote of both houses remove this disability.

Section 4. The validity of the public debt of the United Nations of Earth, authorized by law, including debts incurred for payment of pensions will not be questioned. Neither the United Nations of Earth, nor any member nation, will assume or pay any debt or obligation incurred in the aid of domestic violence, or rebellion against the United Nations of Earth, all such debts are to be held illegal and invalid.

Section 5. The congress will have power to enforce, by appropriate legislation, the provisions of this article.

Article Twenty

The right of the citizens of the United Nations of Earth to vote shall not be denied or abridged by the United Nations of Earth, or by any member nation on account of race, gender, color, previous condition of servitude, religious affiliation, oath, or qualification based on property ownership, payment of taxes, of any kind, or conviction for civil or criminal acts, including treason.

The proposed constitution set forth above is a very close adaption of the US Constitution to our purpose. It is clearly understood that any particular article, sub-section of an article, or word may be rejected, altered, or realigned by those who might be assigned the task of drafting a constitution, in convention, for the purpose of establishing a world government. It may be that those who are delegates to such a convention would wish to designate the United Nations of Earth by another title which would be their prerogative

The proposed constitution is set forth above to allow a detailed discussion from a static base of reference of the problems that are likely to be encountered in establishing a world government that is both efficient and effective. Some general comments are in order before we launch our detailed discussion.

It has been remarked earlier that the current political environment, in relation to the system of nationalism, appears to require that any world government take the form of a republic. The existing system of nation-states cannot under any clearly determined concept be dismantled and then reconstituted under a general federal government. That is to say, it does not make sense to disband the existing nation states and then have a world government reestablish them through its power of delegation. On the other hand, the existing nation states do not seem to be able to generate the needed agreements to handle major global problems such as pandemic disease. In addition, the existing nation states have not been able to generate the type of agreements that would even limit the production and use of military weapons, i.e., they cannot reach even limited agreements concerning disarmament. It is likely that the type of agreements needed to solve these problems will only arise under the auspices of a world government capable of enforcing its own laws. Any organization that was capable of passing and enforcing such laws, even if not a government, would need the power to act as if it were a department in such a government. As a type of incentive it should be recognized that some members of the former Soviet Union did not seek independent nation status but rather joined with Russia in a federation. In addition, it should be pointed out that many European nations have agreed to join in the European Union for at least the obtainment of limited goals. For these reasons it seems inescapable that any world government would be forced to accept a form based on republican principles.

The general world government, as part of a truly republican system, would be constrained to the exercise of the duties and responsibilities directly delegated to it by the constitution. This of course is what would be expected in the case of its initial operations. Subsequent powers may also be given to the general government by further delegations of powers, either officially through amendment of the constitution, or unofficially by means of legislation, executive order, or default delegation by the several nations. It must, however, be pointed out that the only safe way to delegate power to a government is by means of a written constitution as will be pointed out in the analysis of the Federalist Papers. Even the officially delegated powers of government are subject to interpretation by those who are in charge of exercising them. This is particularly true of the judicial branch which has been delegated the official duty of determining the constitutionality of any specific law. As we shall see interpretations can in some cases reverse the original intentions of those who drafted the constitution.

CHAPTER 6. THE FEDERALIST PAPERS AND ARGUMENTS FOR AND AGAINST THE ESTABLISHMENT OF A UNIFIED GOVERNMENT

The Federalist Papers were written with the express purpose of explaining to and convincing those responsible for the ratification of the constitution what was in the various articles of the constitution; and what they were intended to accomplish. In particular, this process was aimed at the state of New York in hope that it would quickly ratify the constitution and become a member of the new union. It should be remembered that seven of the thirteen states had already ratified the constitution prior to their publication. It was evident to everyone that if the state of New York did not ratify the constitution the whole project would fail.

The Federalist Papers, with the proper adaptations, can just as easily be applied to the project of ratifying a new constitution for the establishment of a world government. The same arguments are relevant to each individual's decision to accept or reject such a constitution; and through this acceptance and rejection to each nation's acceptance or rejection of such a constitution, as they were for individuals and states existing in 1790. The principles that underlay the concept of republicanism are the same now as they were in 1790. We have also seen in some detail the points of comparison between existing political conditions and those that existed at the time the US was created. Lastly, just as the Papers were intended to target key states at the time of their publication, they can now be used to target key nations today such as the United States, the Russian Federation, Japan, and China, as well as the European Union.

A detailed look at the content of the Federalist Papers can now be profitably taken up. This will be done using the proposed constitution set forth in Chapter 5 as a basic reference in relation to the arguments presented by the Papers. The Federalist Papers were instilled with the ideas of the enlightenment, as understood in 1789, and it should be kept in mind that the basic principles of the enlightenment are still active factors in today's political environment. The principles of most importance to our concern are the dependence on modern science, and the principles underlying liberal democracy and liberal economics.

The underlying political ideology of the Papers is the enlightenment principles of the promotion of the evolution of modern science, liberal democracy, and liberal economics. Liberal democracy as understood by those who wrote the Papers included the concept of individual human rights protected by the rule of law, representative government under which the people held all sovereign power, and the right to peacefully remove an existing government if deemed necessary, among others. The term liberal economics, as understood in 1789, included the concept of the right to create and maintain private property, a system of relatively free trade, and a minimum of government regulation of the economy as a whole. The evolution of science included the recognition of the benefit to human living standards represented by technology put to practical uses. All of these concepts and many others are found, and applied, in the Papers as the arguments they present in relation to the acceptance or rejection of the proposed constitution.

While the three men who wrote the Papers were all the intellectual children of the enlightenment they were not just academically involved in their understanding of the underlying principles, they were also directly involved in their application in practical affairs. All of them had been actively involved in the drafting of various state constitutions, the Articles of Confederation, and the selection of those who stood as delegates to the constitutional convention. This gave them practical knowledge of the confusions and problems which emerged from the operation of the confederacy and not just theoretical knowledge. They were not only familiar with the constitution of their own states, but were also familiar with all thirteen state constitutions; and they were aware of what had been taken from these constitutions and incorporated into the proposed constitution. They were all in favor of every state ratifying the constitution and, of course, slanted their arguments to accomplish that goal. It is remarkable, however, that the arguments offered with that purpose in mind were limited to a clear, factual, representation of the issues involved and the rational conclusions based on these arguments. In short, the Federalist Papers represented the clearest, most straightforward and honest presentation of the arguments which support liberal democracy that have yet been made, at least, in reference to a written constitution.

The same is to some degree true of the current environment in relation to drafting and ratifying a constitution aimed at establishing a world government. Even though the proposed constitution is largely based on the existing US Constitution the provisions contained in it are also found in many of the written constitutions of other nations. In general, the principles that underlay the enlightenment, enhanced to more closely fit the conditions that exist today, are also a part of the daily operation of nearly every existing nation; that is, every nation has accepted the need for the development of modern science, and the demands of liberal economics especially in relation to the global market. We therefore, begin our discussion with the first number of the Papers.

Number 1 of the Papers has earlier been set forth in its entirety but has not been discussed in any detail. Several passages are specifically related to arguments for a world government but most of this paper is devoted to general arguments justifying the replacement of the confederation with a new government. Although there does not appear to be any danger of the system of nationalism now in place disappearing the arguments in favor of a unified general government are relevant. Hamilton was arguing that from every point of view whether military, financial, or commercial the union would be more efficient and effective than thirteen independent states or two or three regional confederacies. Since these arguments are valid in relation to thirteen independent states and two or three regional confederacies; they are certainly valid for two hundred independent nations or five or six regional confederacies. Currently there are several worldwide organizations in existence the United Nations, the World Bank, the international monetary fund, etc. We have already seen the close similarity of these organizations and the confederation created by the Articles of Confederation. Just as the arguments show that the thirteen states, or two or three regional confederacies would be inadequate to solve the larger problems facing them, that is, the possibility of war between the various states or confederacies, the problems involving trade between the various states, etc.; neither the United Nations, nor the two hundred independent nations, can solve the large problems that face them (the same problems, plus those of pollution, and others). There can be no doubt that the creation of one military capable of maintaining peace will be much more economical than the creation of two hundred, or even five or six. It is also certain that the resolution of commercial disputes can more easily be done with one standard created by law, than by two hundred, or some lesser number, of treaties or other contractual devices. In this sense the decision to constitute a more effective means of handling such problems seems to be just as rational today as it was in 1790.

As we have seen the number goes on to concede that many interests, local institutions, and social standards will be affected by the establishment of a unified government. It was felt that the real danger in this area was to be found in the likelihood of an emotional, rather than a rational, decision concerning the ratification or rejection of the new constitution. This danger is no less real today than it was at the time that this number was written. Human nature is what it is and there is very little that can be done to sway anyone who has taken an emotional stand for or against ratification outside of a patient explanation of one's point of view and the art of gentle persuasion. For example, it is hard to imagine the president of the United States being pleased with the reduction of his office to the current status accorded to state governors. It is equally difficult to imagine those who will lose their positions, not to speak of their livelihood, being pleased with the prospect of the disbandment of the national military organizations. All people that find themselves in such a position, and there will be many of them, a large share of whom will wield a substantial amount of influence within their respective nations, will resist adoption of the new constitution regardless of the public good. Hamilton argued that their interest should be acknowledged and that they should be granted the courtesy of having the best of intentions. Hamilton even cautioned against an uncritical acceptance of the arguments that might be used to counter their resistance. Although this may be very good advice it would be more to the point to have made previous plans as to how those losing their positions, such as those in the national military organizations, will be reabsorbed meaningfully into the economy; and how those who feel a loss of personal status (power, financial, etc) could replace that lost by service in the new general government. The former is undoubtedly the most important in terms of numbers of people involved and the amount of planning needed. At the very least it must be recognized that the resistance to ratification can, and in some cases will be, motivated by ambition, avarice, personal animosity, party oppositions, and other emotion-laden factors. On the other hand, the same emotional factors will also be found in some of those who favor the ratification of the constitution. It can only be hoped that the majority of people find a rational basis for their resistance or acceptance of the new constitution. As mentioned earlier, the main purpose of number 1 of the Papers was to set the stage for the rational arguments that could be presented in favor of ratifying the new constitution.

John Jay is thought to have written number 2 of the Papers, and he begins by conceding that nothing is more necessary than government. Although it may be wished that the world was such a place that government was not needed it is difficult to imagine our world without it. Jay also concedes that regardless of the form of government that is created the people who are a part of that government must grant it some degree of power. The question, for Jay, is whether it is in the interest of the people (here he is speaking directly to the people inhabiting the thirteen states) to grant these powers to only one government or too many. Jay had in mind the dissolution of the existing union under the confederacy into thirteen independent nations or possibly two or three regional confederacies. The arguments set forth in number 2 in favor of one government were, of course, tailored to fit the then existing conditions but can easily be converted to modern conditions.

The crux of Jay's argument is based upon something of a myth in regard to the homogeneity of the populations residing in the thirteen states. Jay, therefore, was responsible for beginning a myth that continues to play an important role in the political ideology of the United States. Although he was undoubtedly only taking into consideration the top three or so percent of the people he saw a distinct homogenous character in the United States. He made it seem that everyone spoke the same language, that every one practiced the same religion (congregational Protestantism), held a belief in representative democracy, and lived with the same manners and customs. This is, of course, in modern times is the core of the WASP myth. In addition, and probably closer to the truth, he identified the patriotic feeling that had arisen with the defeat of the British in the war for independence. This is however not in reality the picture that one would get were they to walk through the thirteen states in 1790. There were African-Americans that spoke many languages, and practiced many religions, had no belief in democracy, and did not have common customs or manners. There were Native Americans who also spoke many languages, practiced many religions, had no concept of democracy, and who did not share common customs or manners. Even when the white population is considered there were some who spoke German, French, Spanish, or other European languages, there were Catholics, Baptists, Congregationalists, etc., there were some who longed to return to the government of a monarchy, and there were an abundance of customs and manners. The point was, however, that those who were responsible for the actual vote within the various states to either ratify or reject the constitution belonged to the upper two or three percent of the population. This group of people fit into Jay's world of homogeneity. This picture drawn by Jay in 1790 has become one of the basic ideological underpinnings of the political unity of the United States. Regardless, however, of the validity of Jay's picture the arguments are still valid in relation to the early US Constitution, as well as, in relation to our project of creating a world government. In our world today the top two or three percent of the population is also very homogenous in just the way that Jay expressed. They tend to use the same language, at least, for business purposes, they tend to have a strong tendency to clearly separate their religion from their politics, they tend to favor democracy, and they share a great deal in common in relation to customs and manners. The rest of the population, however, is as diverse, if not more so, than the population of the early United States. There are Buddhists, Judaists, Muslims, Christians, and many others. There are those who are operating under monarchies, aristocracies, dictatorships, tribal government, theocracies, and more, and there is no way to even begin to label all the differing customs and manners. There is, however, a certain underlying homogeneity in relation to the significant number of people who understand the modern dependence on science, the need for both liberal democracy and liberal economics in support of the global market concept, and of course, the worldwide desire for the benefits of consumerism. At any rate, the arguments set forth in number two of the Papers seem to remain valid.

The desire of the world's people for freedom from fear of external invasion, civil war, and other insurrections is at least as strong as the same desire in the people of the thirteen states that composed the early United States. The need people have to increase their general welfare in terms of education, medical care, the ability to make a living, and to enjoy the fruits of their labor are also the same as those that affected the people of the early United States. In the end, although Jay's arguments concerning homogeneity can be adapted to current conditions, it is maybe more important to recognize that they are unnecessary. The world does, in fact, contain a large number of diverse languages, a significant diversity of religions, and a wide diversity in customs and manners; but does this really matter when the question is whether or not a world government is the best thing for everyone. If the European Union, or for that matter the United Nations, can be used as a model for an argument in favor of world government, the argument would have to be that it does not matter. The United Nations, in particular, has shown that modern technology readily allows for active discussion, real understanding, and practical solutions to a wide range of issues regardless of the above diversity.

In Federalist number 3, again written by John Jay, specific arguments are offered in favor of a unified government. The first and arguably the most important is the argument that all people, regardless of the form of government they live under, have as their foremost goal the attention they give to their personal safety. For the purpose of his argument Jay limits his discussion to safety from invasion by other states or nations and violent internal insurrections. Today it is likely that safety from environmental pollution and fear of weapons of mass destruction would have to be added to the list. The goal of people in regard to safety is the same now as in 1790 but today the people have many more fears some of which could lead to the extinction of the species.

In considering the issue of external invasion, or war generally, Jay accepts the dictum current at the time that wars could be both just and unjust. He does not consider unjust wars as his feeling was that they cannot be prevented but only prepared for as a real danger. He instead concentrates on what at the time were considered to be just wars. He believes just wars to be those that result from a breach of obligations that were created by treaty, or those in defense of direct unprovoked invasion. He points out that the confederation had during its existence concluded treaties with no less than six nations. He argues that it is in the interest of safety that the United States should observe the laws accepted by the international community. He concludes by observing that it would be easier to observe the obligations of treaties and international law if only one versus several governments were involved in making the decisions. He argues that the administration, the political counsels, and the judicial decisions made in reference to these concerns would be wiser, more systematic, and judicious if made by one government rather than two, three, or more governments. This argument was based in part on the belief, on the part of Jay, that better more informed minds would be available for service in the national government than in smaller subdivisions of government.

These arguments when applied to current conditions remain relevant but only when altered to a considerable degree. It is, for example, still relevant to consider the importance of observation of treaty obligations as they are still one of the main causes of conflict. It would be true, however, that if a world government or union were to be established that there would no longer be any treaties per se. However, the same causes of dispute would still exist, that is, there would be disputes over the fulfillment of contractual obligations, there would be disputes over territory, and there would be disputes over immigration, etc. etc. These disputes would still have to be resolved and Jay's argument that consistency, systematic treatment, and more flexible standards would all result from the use of law versus the use of treaties. There also would no longer be a need for international law as it would be replaced with a court system created along the lines of that which functions within the United States. Again, there would still be a need for a final arbitrator to settle the disputes that were outlined above. Instead of an international court of justice this role would be filled by a Supreme Court and whatever lower courts the world congress deemed necessary. Whether or not unified world government would lead to better more informed minds being brought into service is debatable. Initially this did appear to happen in the case of the early US but it is at least questionable whether the same results are now to be found. The same may be true of any world government formed unless there is some incentive for the best most informed minds to enter public service. It is, however, certain that people will still put forth the vast majority of their effort in the attempt to enhance their personal safety. It is equally certain that one effective government would more easily accomplish this task than two hundred or even two or three. One needs only to look at the record amassed by the fifty states of the US public in regard to external invasion and violent internal insurrection to see the validity of the argument. Direct violence by any one nation or group of nations under a world government would be treated as an internal juridical issue to be resolved by arbitration by the Supreme Court once the violence had been quelled.

Any number of conflicts currently in progress could, upon the institution of a world government, come under pressure from the general government to submit to final arbitration of the differences involved or in fact be forced to end the violence. For example, the conflict between the Sudanese government and the tribal peoples of Darfur is not only a military question but a moral question. The world government would be negligent if it did not immediately commit the forces necessary to end the killing; but it would be equally negligent if it did not at the same time offer a civil process of arbitration to settle the outstanding issues.

In all cases but one, the federal government of the US has been able to defuse all cases of internal insurrection. Unfortunately, however, the US has not also been able to force a civil solution to the problems that underlay those insurrections in the first place. The violence has been contained but the problems remain unsolved and are simmering on the back burner. Debates over how far to extend the rights of women, the rights of gays, the rights of the handicapped, and the rights of the underprivileged, all need to be addressed at the civil level, but this effort would have to be made by the federal and state governments in concert. Whether or not government is the best choice for the solution of such problems as racial discrimination, religious discrimination, ethnic discrimination, and others is debatable at the very least. It is the hearts of the people that must be altered in these cases, not the law.

In the case of true civil war, that is, where one or more nations attempt to withdraw from the union, as was the case in the United States, or where one faction within a nation is attempting to overthrow the existing government, another problem exists. In these cases, there may be some reason to truly consider whether or not the complaints that have led to this situation are just or unjust. It is certainly possible, for example, that those attempting to overthrow the existing government within any specific nation have the support of the majority of the people. It may also be the case that the existing government for one reason or another is repressing the civil rights of the population. In these cases, the general government if requested by the affected nation could enter into a military action to quell the violence.

It should be recognized, however, that quelling the violence does nothing to eradicate the underlying problems. The civil court system should be immediately opened to the two parties for the public airing of the issues involved and the resolution of the issues if possible. In some cases it might be ordered that the existing government be replaced by a sponsored election conducted within the nation affected. In other cases the complaining parties may be required to enter into some type of compromise solution with the existing government remaining intact. In some situations it may even be necessary to split the existing nation into two separate and independent nations. In the situation where one or more nations wishes to voluntarily withdraw from the union the problem is so serious that in many cases the total dissolution of the union may be at hand. It can, of course, be written into the constitution that the several nations are denied the right to voluntarily withdraw from the union for any reason. This, of course, will not stop those nations who feel justified in their wish to withdraw; and will require the remainder of the union to apply force to prevent it. This is what happened in the case of the US civil war. There would be one major difference between the two cases. In the case of the US civil war the eleven states that withdrew from the union had the capability of immediately fielding a military comparably equipped with that which the union could present. They were also capable of fielding a military comparable if not superior to that of the union in terms of military leadership. If the general world government is established with a total disarmament of the member nations then there would not be any comparable military power available to the withdrawing nations, that is to say, that military power would be preponderantly in favor of the union. The same would likely be true of the military leadership. It would, therefore, be possible for the union to force membership upon those wishing to withdraw but forcing membership would not remove the causes that brought about the wish to withdraw. In the end irreconcilable issues might lead to the withdrawal of a nation or group of nations from the union. In this case the remaining members of the union would be put in a position similar to that which exists with the US today, that is; they would be forced to rely on the general government to conduct relations with the nations that had split off from the union.

In the latter case set forth above it would again be necessary to reestablish international law and the obligations found in treaties and other contractual agreements. The real danger here would be that the bargaining position of the world union would be so great that the nations that remained outside the union even if gathered into some type of confederacy might not be able to obtain just agreements. For example, it is not likely that if the world union had entered onto a path to bring about the cessation of emissions into the atmosphere to end the manmade contributions to climate change that the world government would allow the nations outside the union to continue to pollute the atmosphere. In such cases the bargaining power of the general union would be so great as to deny any independent right to the nations outside the union. It is also possible to foresee a situation involving the confederation of all Islamic nations and their desire to remain outside the world union on the basis of their religious tenets. The position that these nations hold in relation to the world's natural resources, especially oil, would make it imperative that the general union negotiate treaties with them, at least until the union was capable of totally eliminating its dependence on oil. In this case the confederacy might have the preponderance of bargaining power on its side and be capable of forcing unjust contractual obligations on the general union. Although such a scenario is still theoretical it is possible as even today a radical branch of Islam is calling for the total confederation of Islamic nations to be governed by Islamic law. If all nations were to join the general union it goes without saying that there would be no need for treaties or international law as all disputes, of whatever nature, would be handled internally through the general court system as in the current US

In relation to the overwhelming desire of most people to be free from violence to their persons, or to their property, the control of criminal behavior is much more pervasive than the control of internal insurrection. The number of people in the current US that suffer violence to their person from criminal acts, such as assault and battery, rape, and robbery is greatly misunderstood. The numbers are very large even in the counties that claim the least in rate of crime. Those that suffer violence to their property from crimes such as robbery, fraud, and corporate manipulation are also found in large numbers. It is assumed in our case that each nation will retain the right to establish and maintain a competent policing organization to deal with internal crime. It is also assumed the general government will have power to operate a policing organization separate from the military to enforce its own laws, as well as, to aid in the control of crime that crosses national boundaries such as the drug trade. The problem, however, is that this type of system has been in effect in the US for the whole of its history and yet the US has one of the highest crime rates in the world. It can, therefore, be argued that the current system for dealing with the problems of criminal behavior is not satisfactory and that it would be wise to allow the development of alternatives to the current system. This, however, would be outside the scope of the constitution, that is, whatever system is developed to handle criminal behavior the constitution can do no more than to delegate the power of policing to the various governmental institutions. In one particular case it is necessary to consider the separation of the issues involved from the actions taken. In the case of terrorism (in particular the tenets of the US "war on terrorism") it must be recognized that the terrorists are in fact insurgents. This clearly means that they are involved with the attempt to replace a government that they believe to be repressive in connection with their civil rights. This represents the issues of terrorism. Insurrectionists groups have taken the approach of committing violent actions to bring attention to the issues they hold important in many cases these acts occur outside of the country in which the insurrection is occurring. The world government in league with the national governments must quell the violent acts but also must address the issues involved in a just manner.

John Jay is also believed to have written numbers 4 and 5 of the Federalist Papers. In combination they represent an extension of the arguments Jay considered in numbers 2 and 3. They are, of course, again directed at strengthening a favorable attitude towards ratification of the constitution. They do not add anything of substance to our discussion that has not already been covered in considerable detail beforehand.

Alexander Hamilton wrote number 6 of the Papers and exemplifies an insight into human nature that is clearly exhibited in the current system of nationalism. The arguments are no doubt specific to the events of 1789 but they are easily extended to comparable events that are occurring in today's world. Because of the nature of the insight exhibited by Hamilton it will be worthwhile to set forth number 6 in its entirety.

> The three last numbers of this paper have been dedicated to an enumeration of the dangers to which we should be exposed, in a state of disunion, from the arms and arts of foreign nations. I shall now proceed to delineate dangers of a different and, perhaps, still more alarming kind-those which will in all probability flow from dissensions between the states themselves, and from domestic factions and convulsions. These have been already in some instances slightly anticipated; but they deserve a more particular and full investigation.

> A man must be far gone in utopian speculations who can seriously doubt that, if these states should either be wholly disunited, or only united in partial confederacies, the subdivisions into which they might be thrown would have frequent and violent contests with each other. To presume a want of motives for such contests as an argument against their existence, would be to forget that men are ambitious, vindictive, and rapacious. To look for a continuation of harmony between a number of independent, unconnected sovereignties in the same neighborhood, would be to disregard the uniform course of human events, and to set at defiance the accumulated experience of the ages.

The causes of hostility among nations are innumerable. There are some which have a general and almost constant operation upon the collective bodies of society. Of this description are the love of power or the desire of pre-eminence and dominion, the jealousy of power, or the desire of equality and safety. There are others which have a more circumscribed though equally operative influence within their spheres. Such are the rival ships and competitions of commerce between commercial nations. And there are others, not less numerous than either of the former, which take their origin entirely in private passions, in the attachments, enmities, interests, hopes, and fears of leading individuals in the communities of which they are members. Men of this class, whether the favorites of a king or of a people, have in too many instances abused the confidence they possessed; and assuming the pretext of some public motive, have not scrupled to sacrifice the national tranquility to personal advantage in personal gratification.

The celebrated Pericles, in compliance with the resentment of a prostitute, at the expense of much of the blood and treasure of his countrymen, attacked, vanquished, and destroyed the city of the *Samnians*. The same man, stimulated by private pique against the *Megarengians*, another nation of Greece, or to avoid a prosecution with which he was threatened as an accomplice in a supposed theft of the statuary Phidias, or to get rid of the accusations prepared to be brought against him for dissipating the funds of the state in the purchase of popularity, or from a combination of all these causes, was the primitive author of that famous and fatal war, distinguished in the Grecian annals the name of the *Peloponnesian war*; which, after various vicissitudes, intermissions, and renewals, terminated in the ruin of the Athenian commonwealth.

The ambitious Cardinal, who was prime minister to Henry VIII, permitting his vanity to aspire to the triple crown, entertained hopes of succeeding in the acquisition of that splendid prize by the influence of the emperor Charles V. To secure the favor and interest of this enterprising and powerful monarch, he precipitated England into a war with France, contrary to the plainest dictates of policy, and at the hazard of the safety and independence, as well of the kingdom over which he presided by his counsels, as of Europe in general. For if there ever was a sovereign who bid fair to realize the project of universal monarchy, it was the Emperor Charles V, of whose intrigues Wolsey was at one the instrument and the dupe.

The influence which the bigotry of one female, the petulance of another, and cabals of a third, had in the contemporary policy, ferments, and pacifications, of a considerable part of Europe, are topics that have been too often descanted upon not to be generally known.

To multiply examples of the agency of personal considerations in the production of great national events, either foreign or domestic, according to their direction, would be an unnecessary waste of time. Those who have but a superficial acquaintance with the sources from which they are drawn will themselves recollect a variety of instances; and those who have a tolerable knowledge of human nature will not stand in need of such lights, to form their opinion either of the reality or extent of that agency.

Perhaps, however, a reference, tending to illustrate the general principle, may with propriety be made to a case which has lately happened among ourselves. If Shays had been a *desperate debtor*, it is much to be doubted whether Massachusetts would have been plunged into a civil war.

But notwithstanding the concurring testimony of experience, in this particular, there are still to be found visionary or designing men, who stand ready to advocate the paradox of perpetual peace between states, though dismembered and alienated from each other. The genius of repub-lics (say they) is pacific; the spirit of commerce has a tendency to soften the manners of men, and to extinguish those inflammable humours which have so often kindled into wars. Commercial republics, like ours, will never be disposed to waste themselves in ruinous contentions with each other. They will be governed by mutual interest, and will cultivate a spirit of mutual amity and concord.

Is it not (we may ask these projectors in politics) the true interest of all nations to cultivate the same benevolent and philosophic spirit? If this be their true interest, have they in fact pursued it? Has it not, on the contrary, invariably been found that momentary passions, and immediate interests, have a more active and imperious control over human conduct than gen-eral and remote considerations of policy, utility, or justice? Have republics in practice been less addicted to war than monarchies? Are not the former administered by men as well as the latter? Are there not aversions, predict lections, rivalships, and desires of unjust acquisitions, that affect nations as well as kings? Are not popular assemblies frequently subject to the impulses of rage, resentment, jealousy, avarice, and of other irregular and violent propensities? Is it not well known that their determinations are often governed by a few individuals in whom they place confidence, and are, of course, liable to be tinctured by the passions, and views of those in-dividuals? Has commerce hitherto done anything more than changed the object of war? Is not the love of wealth as domineering and enterprising a passion as that of power and glory? Have there not been as many wars founded upon commercial motives since that has become the prevailing system of nations, as were before occasioned by the cupidity of territory or dominion? Has not the spirit of commerce, in many instances, admin-istered new incentives to the appetite, both for the one and for the other? Let experience, the least fallible guide of human opinions, be appealed to for an answer to these inquiries.

Sparta, Athens, Rome, and Carthage were all republics; two of them, Athens and Carthage, of the commercial kind. Yet were they as often en-gaged in wars, offensive and defensive, as the neighboring monarchies of the same times. Sparta was little better than a well-regulated camp; and Rome was never sated of carnage and conquest.

Carthage, though a commercial republic, was the aggressor in the very war that ended in her destruction. Hannibal had carried her arms into the heart of Italy, and to the gates of Rome, before Scipio, in turn, gave him an overthrow in the territories of Carthage, and made a conquest of the commonwealth.

Venice, in later times, figured more than once in wars of ambition, till, becoming an object to the other Italian states; Pope Julius II found the means to accomplish that formidable league which gave a deadly blow to the power and pride of this haughty republic.

The provinces of Holland, till they were overwhelmed in debts and taxes, took a leading and conspicuous part in the wars of Europe. They had furious contests with England for the dominion of the sea, and were among the most preserving and most implacable of opponents to Louis XIV.

In the government of Britain the representatives of the people compose one branch of the national legislature. Commerce has been for ages the predominant pursuit of that country. Few nations, nevertheless, have been more frequently engaged in war; and the wars in which that kingdom has been engaged have, in numerous instances, proceeded from the people.

There have been, if I may so express it, almost as many popular as royal wars. The cries of the nation and the importunities of their representatives have, upon various occasions, dragged their monarchs into war, or continued them in it, contrary to their inclinations, and sometimes contrary to the real interests of the state. In that memorable struggle for superiority between the rival houses of *Austria* and *Bourbon*, which so long kept Europe in a flame, it is well known that the antipathies of the English against the French, seconding the ambition, or rather the avarice, of a favorite leader, protracted the war beyond the limits marked out by sound policy, and for a considerable time in opposition to the views of the court.

The wars of these two last-mentioned nations have in a great measure grown out of commercial considerations. The desire of supplanting and the fear of being supplanted, either in particular branches of traffic or in the general advantages of trade and navigation.

From this summary of what has taken place in other countries, whose situations have borne the nearest resemblance to our own, what reason can we have to confide in those reveries which would seduce us into an expectation of peace and cordiality between members of the present confederacy, in a state of separation? Have we not already seen enough of the fallacy and extravagance of those idle theories which have amused us with the promises of an exemption from the imperfections, weaknesses, and evils incident to society in every shape? Is it not time to awaken from the deceitful dream of a golden age, and to adopt as a practical maxim for the direction of our political conduct that we, as well as the other inhabitants of the globe, are yet remote from the happy empire of perfect wisdom and perfect virtue?

Let the point of extreme depression to which our national dignity and credit have sunk, let the inconveniences felt everywhere from a lax and ill administration of government, let the revolt of a part of the state of North Carolina, the late menacing disturbances in Pennsylvania, and the actual insurrections and rebellions in Massachusetts declare ____!

So far is the general sense of mankind from corresponding with the tenets of those who endeavor to lull asleep our apprehensions of discord and hostility between the states, in the event of disunion, that it has from long observation of the progress of society become a sort of axiom in politics, that vicinity, or nearness of situation, constitutes nations natural enemies. An intelligent writer expresses himself on this subject to this effect: 'NEIGHBORING nations [says he] are naturally enemies of each other, unless their common weakness forces them to league in a CONFEDERATIVE REPUBLIC, and their constitution prevents the secret jealousy which disposes all states to aggrandize themselves at the expense of their neighbors.' This passage at the same time points out the EVIL and suggests the REMEDY.[1] (Publius)

There is little that can be added to the psychological insight exhibited by Hamilton. Many more modern examples to the same effect could be enumerated but are not necessary. It is of interest that Hamilton takes a very modern approach in assigning the same strength and weakness that exist in human nature and applies them to the relations that exist between nations.

In particular, a world increasingly dominated by the commercialization of the global market place has brought to the forefront many of the psychological traits expressed by Hamilton. Little has changed since 1789 that would make it less likely that nations will desire to supplant, and will desire to resist being supplanted in relation to their existing position in the global market. There also can be little doubt that the control of natural resources, financial institutions, and other commercially based policy decisions will continue to grow in importance, especially in relation to the production of disputes between the competing nations. In this sense the conclusion drawn by Hamilton that a unified government presents the best hope of waylaying these problems is also applicable to the current world environment.

In number 7 of the papers Hamilton moves from the general arguments of number 6 to arguments specifically relating to the situation of the thirteen states. He begins with the fact that the thirteen states when they had been English colonies had obtained title to what was then known as the western lands (essentially the Ohio and Tennessee Valley's). When the thirteen states had agreed to accept the Articles of Confederation they had voluntarily ceded their claims to this land to the general government. If the union were to be dissolved the claims of the various states would be revived. This would be resisted not only by any state that had no claim to this land, but also by the people who resided in these areas. There was little doubt in Hamilton's mind that such claims could, and probably would, lead to military contests between the competing interests. He also speaks of the disputes that would arise in commercial areas, such as the implementation

---

1 *The Federalist* Pgs 38-41, Great Books of the Western World, Encyclopedia Britannica.

of import and export duties, the control of ports, and the taxation on products traveling in interstate trade. These were all potential problems that were a part of the ruling classes' general knowledge and needed little explanation. The same is probably true of the ruling classes that today control the various nations. Little needs to be said about the causes that are responsible for the wars that are now raging, that is, they are territorial, personal, commercial, and all the other reasons set forth above. In short, just as in 1789 the various philosophical and psychological factors that are relevant should be taken into consideration in the attempt to form a rational decision concerning the ratification or rejection of a potential constitution initiating a world government.

Number 8 and 9 were also written by Hamilton, and they extend the vision he had of a world in which thirteen independent nations replaced the existing confederacy. Secondly, a beginning is made in the consideration of the effective scope of a confederacy. He raises this last issue in response to an objection that had been raised to adoption of the new constitution. The crux of the objection was that the large extent of territory of the proposed United States, and the size of its population, made an effective union impossible. He begins by arguing that there is nothing in precedent, or in the principles of representative government, that naturally limits the size of a confederacy. It is interesting to note that any serious discussion of the possibility of a world government always raises these very issues. It is usually stated without equivocation that the size of the world, its massive population, and the diversity of its cultures make a unified world government impossible. In Hamilton's time the confederacy of Lycia was cited as an example of the opposite conclusion. In our time Great Britain, the United States, the Russian Federation, China, and India can all be cited as examples of confederations that have incorporated very large territories, large populations, and significant culture diversity. As in Hamilton's time, there is today nothing evident in the principles of representative democracy that makes a world union impossible. This union could, and probably would, include the vast majority of nations that now exist, as well as, incorporating lands now common to all such as Antarctica.

The current operation of the European Union, although constituted for less extensive purposes than a general government, stands as a recent example of the high level of cooperation that can be obtained by modern confederacies. It has been in the main successful in bringing about extensive cooperation in inter-nation trade, a unified monetary system, and political homogeneity on the front of world opinion. This union, if adapted to assume the responsibility of a government would stand as a good model for the structuring of a world union.

Number 10 of the papers, also written by Hamilton, is one of the most important of all in respect to any attempt to establish an effective world union. The objection presented and treated in number 10 is that the liberty expected to be practiced under a representative democracy results from the formation of distinct or conflicting interests. These interests include, but are not limited to, those of debtors versus creditors, propertied interests versus the interest of those without property, manufacturing interests versus commercial interests, Protestant versus Catholic, etc. The danger arises when one type of interest is able to garner control of the legislative and judicial functions of the government and use them to enhance their interests at the expense of the rest of society. Hamilton accepts that divergent interests are an inherent part of representative democracy, as they are in any form of government, and contends that this must be so if liberty is to remain a vital part of society. Since the evolution of varying interests (one can, if desired, assign these interests to the various classes that exist within any society) within a representative democracy cannot be eliminated, the only recourse is for the society to control them. Hamilton's argument is based on the belief that the larger a society is, when governed by a representative democracy, the less likely it is that any one interest will represent a majority of the power. This can clearly be shown to have been the case in Great Britain, the United States, and the European Union. He continues to point out that what represents a dominant even passionate interest in one part of the society normally will not also be an interest that dominates the rest of society. In most cases the majority represented by the rest of society will prevent a minority interest from exerting itself within society; although over time it may become the majority interest if it is based upon the public good. It is also possible that a minority interest may represent injustice and act against the public good yet still become the majority interest within society. It has, however, been the case that when such interests do control society for a time they are soon dismissed from public service and replaced with more compatible interests.

The eighteenth amendment to the US Constitution is a good example of the above principle. A minority reform movement was able to garner enough support among the several states to pass an amendment banning the use and sale of alcohol in the United States. The reaction of the public (presumably the "silent majority") was to consciously break the law and continue to use and buy alcohol. The interest of the majority became so clear over a period of years that another amendment was passed repealing the former amendment. A necessary component of the ability to overthrow unjust interests, or interests that go against the public good, is the ability to peacefully replace them.

It is likely that a union composed of all the existing nations into a world union, upheld by principles of representative democracy, would extend even less opportunity for any one interest to dominate the whole of society. Such a union would also increase the unlikelihood that any one interest could act in subversion of justice or the public good. In part a later argument will attempt to show how the two hundred plus year history of the US supports this argument. An attempt will be made, in other words, to show how the development of a two party system, the growth of interest groups, and the decay of personal responsibility in the individual citizen have affected the operation of a representative democracy in the case of the US

In number 11 Hamilton begins the discussion of the commercial arguments that favor adoption of the new constitution. All of the arguments he presents are specifically related to the conditions that existed in 1790 and apply only to nation-states as entities. In this sense they offer little that is of use in the discussion of world government. One of the major issues facing the world's nations today, however, is the commercial ramifications of a global market. In 1790 the closest approach to a global market was represented by Great Britain's domination of the world's oceans. The majority of the people, whether living in a nation-state, or not, were in some way affected by the English monopoly. In some cases, as that of the US, they were colonies and in other cases they were markets for the obtaining of raw materials or for selling finished products. It was the English monopoly of trade through its control of the seas that Hamilton wished to see come to an end. He was convinced that the only way such a monopoly could be broken was for the thirteen states to unite into a commercial union. Today's global market consists of more players than the three large players of 1790 but the game is still pretty much the same. After World War II Great Britain, France, and Holland all lost their colonial empires. Spain had lost its empire by 1920. The United States by this time represented almost seventy per cent of the total trade worldwide and controlled the lion's share of the financial and manufacturing industries throughout the world. It was not long, however, until this hegemony was challenged by the rise of Germany, Japan, and later the European Union. Today a few countries such as the United States, Japan, and the members of the European Union control most of the world's manufacturing products, that is to say, these countries are responsible for most of the manufactured products traded on the world market either through their internal industries or through their control of outsourced products. They also, between them, are responsible for most of the use of the world's natural resources. Lastly, they represent a virtual monopoly on products that require intensive, high capital, manufacturing processes such as high tech microprocessors, automobiles, airplanes, etc. The rest of the nations are either markets for the products produced by these countries, or sources of the natural resources that they need, or lastly, the source of the cheap labor needed to outsource the work that cannot be accomplished by the outworn internal industrial complex. On the bleak side they are also responsible for the majority of environmental pollution. Other nations, however, also compete on the world market through the development of non-labor intensive, low capital, but highly flexible businesses, such as clothing, jewelry, and others. The European Union and the Far Asian Rim associations were created specifically to break down the monopoly of the United States; just as the importation of the industrial revolution into the early US was intended to break down the monopoly held by Great Britain. The incorporation of the world's nations into a unified government would have the same effect as the creation of the United States and the European Union. Both resulted in the elimination of most if not all import and export duties among themselves, elimination of all border restrictions between themselves, the use of a unified monetary system, and the ability to make joint decisions especially of a commercial nature in their best interest, among other advantages. The two organizations were no longer subject internally to production quotas and other unilateral trade restrictions. Each individual nation in the case of the European Union was able to concentrate on the products most conducive to its circumstances and was allowed access to an unrestricted market to sell them. In short, a world union if effective would create a worldwide domestic market similar to that which exists in the United States and the European Union. There would be relatively unrestricted trade between the several nations but there would not be a global market as understood today. Each member nation would also have the benefit of a unified monetary standard, a standard system of weights and measures, and uniform regulations concerning product quality, distribution, and warranty. Each nation would also be subject to uniform regulations concerning the use and availability of the world's natural resources, the control of pollution, and safety inspections. This aspect of a world union would of course be a very sensitive issue for the United States, the European Union, China, Japan, India, and a few others who have in one way or another captured a sizable share of the global market. All these nations are attempting to cope with the various issues that have arisen in relation to the global market through treaty negotiations. Some success has been noted but in most areas the problems have been pushed to the back burner rather being solved. It is likely that a world union would be as successful, if not more so, in regulating world trade as has been the United States and the European Union within their respective unions.

In number 12 Hamilton opens the issue of providing revenue powers to the general government. Without saying anything further concerning Hamilton's arguments it is clearly recognized that the general government would be granted the power to independently maintain its day-to-day operations. The question is how to limit the revenue powers of the general government to the accomplishment of this task. Obviously, the revenue would be raised by the imposition of taxes, however, the issues of uniform application, uniform enforcement, uniform collection, and the determination of what taxes would still remain to be answered. It is likely that some form of direct taxation, whether the sole province of the general government, or concurrent with the national governments, would be the best solution.

There also appear to be several issues that would need to be settled by the convention before an effort could be made to determine what taxes are to be used. First, a determination at least in the form of an estimate must be made as to the amount of revenue likely to needed by the general government. It is also likely that a similar process would be carried out on the national level in relation to a yearly budget minus what is now spent on the various military budgets. Each nation under normal circumstances determines its revenue needs by determining the cost of the services it is expected to render and the cost of delivering these services. These services are split between military, welfare, infrastructure, education, and other services. The largest share currently in most nations is for the military and welfare payments. With total disarmament the total revenue is likely to be shared largely by welfare payments, the cost of the civil bureaucracy, the creation and maintenance of infrastructure, education, and public sanitation and water supplies. Under a world union the welfare, infrastructure, sanitary and water systems, and others would be shared by all levels of government. This would result in a vast increase in the amounts spent on education, health care, old age pensions, disability payments, as well as, on roads, bridges, water systems, and sanitary disposal systems which would also now include the safe disposal of toxic waste. It is to be expected that a flat rate income tax would be the best source of revenue for the general government. It would allow for uniformity of implementation, uniformity of enforcement, uniformity of collection, and allow for the use of the already existing systems of national collection methods. It goes without saying, however, that such a tax would only give these benefits if it was implemented without any exceptions of any nature. It is also likely that, at least initially, a certain level of minimum income would be necessary before the tax would be accessed. Lastly, some method of fairly allocating the funds available to the general government would need to be instituted to insure a just distribution based upon real need.

The source of revenue, both for the general government, and for the national governments, and their various sub-divisions, is a separate question from the amount of revenue needed. It will be the duty of the convention to specifically provide for the sources of revenue available to the general government. As stated above one such source would be a flat rate income tax. This tax could be concurrent with the same type of tax being assessed by the National governments as is the case in most of the states of the United States. The various national governments, as well as their local subdivisions, would then be allowed sole use of sales and property taxes. Luxury taxes, various sin taxes, inspection fees, pollution taxes, etc. are all sources of available revenue for the appropriate government. There is no fear, however, that in one way or another needed revenue will be raised; the problem is to insure that it is raised in a just manner.

In number 13 Hamilton faces the issue that the expected size of the general government would be too expensive to maintain. He accurately points out that the cost of the general government, regardless of its size, could not be more expensive than the maintenance of thirteen, or two or three, such governments. Whatever responsibilities and duties are granted solely to the general government at that point those duties and responsibilities no longer need to be funded by the national governments. For example, assigning the sole duty of regulating inter-nation trade to the general government relieves the national governments of maintaining their own bureaucracy for that purpose.

Whether or not the various duties and responsibilities initially given to the national and local governments will tend to gravitate to the general government over time as they did in the United States remains to be seen. In each case where a national or local government power is taken over by the general government the need for additional revenue is proportionate. It is hoped that each nation as well as its various local subdivisions will be willing to retain within their own power control over the social, cultural, and religious attributes that make them unique. In the end the powers that are retained by the national governments, and their local sub-divisions, is determined by the amount of individual responsibility their citizens are willing to assume as does liberty generally.

Number 14, written by James Madison ends the general discussion in favor of ratification of the constitution. Madison once again approaches the objection that the size of the proposed government, the country, and the population, especially as a representative democracy, would be impossible. Madison's response was to point out that the rapid growth of science and technology had provided much better roads, canals, and other improvements concerning the ability to travel and communicate that the problem had been negated. This was not totally true in 1790 and is not true today either. Problems of logistics do remain. However, it is even more likely today than in 1790 that science and technology will have the capability of greatly reducing these problems if not totally eliminating them.

Today the issue of travel and the ability to keep ones constituents informed is not likely to be even raised. This does not mean that the same issue will not be raised in some other form, such as the inability to maintain separate cultural diversities under a world union.

Chapter 7. How Much Power or Sovereignty Should Be Given to the World Government?

Hamilton in number fifteen opens the examination of the reasons that can be offered concerning the ineffectiveness of the current union under the Articles of Confederation. The arguments presented although not strictly analogous are cogent in a consideration of the purposes for which the United Nations was established. One quotation from the paper is adequate to establish the analogy between the Articles of Confederation and the United Nations Charter.

> The great and radical vice in the construction of the existing confederation is in the principle of legislation for STATES or GOVERNMENTS, in their CORPORATE CAPACITIES, and as contradistinquished from INDIVIDUALS of which they consist. Though this principle does not run through all the powers delegated to the union, yet it pervades and governs those on which the efficacy of the rest depends. Except as to the rule of apportionment, the United States has an indefinite discretion to make requisitions for men and money; but they have no authority to raise either, by regulations extending to the individual citizens of America. The consequence of this is that though in theory their resolutions concerning objects are laws, constitutionally binding on the members of the union, yet in practice they are mere recommendations which the states observe or disregard at their option.[1] No better description of the position of the United Nations could have been written today. From this quote it is obvious that the status quo clearly involves the United Nations, under its current charter, in all the ineffectiveness that was apparent under the Articles of Confederation. Each nation can, and does, either accept or reject the resolutions (mandates) of the United Nations as its interests dictate.

---

1 *The Federalist Papers*, No. 15, p. 64, Great Books of the Western World, Encyclopedia Britannica.

In number 16, Hamilton argues the logical conclusions that can be drawn from the lack of power to enforce laws, regulations, or mandates, regardless of the type, or form, of government involved. Although the arguments used by Hamilton are specifically targeted to the lack of powers under the Articles they could just as easily have been written with the U.N. charter in mind. The comparison Hamilton makes between the Articles and the new US Constitution could also be made between the U.N. charter and the proposed world constitution contained herein without exception. The point being that regardless of the justice, or the good provided for the general welfare, the laws passed by the two organizations, i.e., the Confederacy and the United Nations, cannot be left to the caprice of the individual states or nations for enforcement and be effective. They must instead be capable of independently enforcing the laws they pass in relation to the individuals that they expect to apply them to (and for). The importance of number 16 in relation to world government cannot be overstated. It can only be recommended that anyone who is in favor of effective world government pay particular attention to this number, especially in relation to the future of any organization based upon a treaty of friendship, such as the current United Nations.

In number 17, Hamilton approaches the concept of the importance of granting the general government the power to affect directly the citizens of which it is composed. While the arguments are largely based on the example of early modern governing techniques they still are in some degree applicable to our current situation. The confederacy is compared to the monarch while the states that compose the union are compared to the various baronies. The people or citizens of the confederacy are compared to the serfs of Europe. The monarch, under normal conditions, is seen as barely capable of ruling the various baronies, and totally removed from any direct power over the serfs. The confederacy is seen to also be incapable of ruling over the states that compose the union and to have no direct relationship with the citizens of the various states. In our current situation the United Nations stands in the relation of the confederacy in relation to the nations, that is, it is incapable of governing them. It also has no direct influence or power in relation to the citizens of the various nations. The nations that currently exist are totally independent sovereign nations with absolute control over their own citizens. In the case of the United Nations the treaty of friendship was concluded with no intention of creating a world government, or any other type of governmental institution, in the United Nations. Whether or not the citizens of the various nations expected to be relieved of any duties or responsibilities they owed to the nation they resided in they were not given that choice. The current situation in the world of nationalism is very clearly set forth by Hamilton and Madison in numbers 18, 19, and 20.

Number 18 is an interesting excursion into the history of representative democracy. While it is true that this excursion at times is tedious one important lesson can be taken from it. The lesson is that the liberty of any given society of people depends, to a great degree, upon the institutions that exist, or they create, to protect it. In our world there are people who proudly proclaim that they are free while others are struggling violently to become free and yet others live in ignorance of the fact that they are not free in any meaningful sense of the word. The point being made is that a confederacy cannot be effective if the constituent members retain all their sovereign powers. Effective government cannot result from leaving the individual members the power to accept or reject the laws that were the purpose of the confederacy in the first place. The ineffectiveness, as pointed out in number 18, of the German, Polish, and Swiss confederacies in 1789 are cases to the point. The United Nations, OPEC, the European Union and other such confederacies are examples from the modern environment. Just as the Federalist Papers held that the US could not be effective under these conditions the world government also would not be effective under them, that is to say, for a world government to be effective it must have independent sovereign power.

One of the main objections to the ratification of the constitution centered on the fear that the general government would be given so much sovereign power as to quickly degenerate into a tyranny. The same objection has been offered each time a serious call has been made to reform the United Nations into an effective sovereign organization. In 1790 the proposed constitution, in all likelihood, was the first document that attempted to divide sovereign power between a general government of the union and its members. In this case it was a division of powers between the federal government of the US and the thirteen member states. In our case it would be between the general government of the United Nations of Earth and the member nations. In the US, the actual division of powers was tripartite, i.e., the power was divided between the general and state governments with the remainder being reserved to the people (governmental sub-divisions of the states). The same would be true in our case also. The history of the US points out that, at the very least, it is possible to successfully divide sovereign power among a number of independent governments. It can be argued that the subsequent history of the US indicates that it is also true that the slow evolution of power in the federal government through various means also evidenced at the same time the diminishing of power in the individual states. There is no way, of course, to determine in advance whether or not the history of a world government would parallel that of the US simply because it was modeled after the US

In numbers 21 and 22 Hamilton addresses what he sees to be the major defects of the Articles of Confederation. We have covered these in detail above but it still might be profitable to review them once again. First, the confederacy was not given independent power to enforce the laws passed by the US legislative body making the laws essentially recommendations to the states. Second, the confederacy was not given the means to independently raise revenue. The general government was given the power to make a budget and to requisition these funds from the member states; but did not have the power to compel payment. Third, the confederacy was not given the power to create and maintain an independent military. The general government, therefore, was not in a position to prevent the invasion of any state, or group of states, by another state, or group of states, or by a foreign power. The general government was also powerless to quell any violent insurrections that might arise within the borders of any individual state. These are the three defects that Hamilton saw as the most important under the Articles and he pointed out that the constitution intended to repair all three of them. The same situation exists with the United Nations as has been pointed out a number of times above. It goes without saying that any government that will be effective in today's world will have to be able to enforce its laws, sustain a military capable of preventing invasion and insurrection, be capable of financing itself independent of the goodwill of the members, and to maintain a peaceful resolution of trade disputes between its members, and itself and foreign governments. This would, except for the latter, be true of an effective world government.

Hamilton also set forth several defects that he considered to less vital than the three set forth above. First, he felt that because the general government could not independently enforce its laws that it could not effectively regulate the commercial activities between the states and between the states and foreign nations. In this area Hamilton felt that regulations issued by the general government, as well as, formal laws, must also be capable of being enforced through the judicial system to be effective. Second, Hamilton pointed out that the use of one vote for each member of the union in regard to the actions of the general government was patently unfair. He felt that it was not only unfair, but unjust, that a small state, such as Rhode Island should have an equal say in the union with a large state, such as New York. He points out that even using a majority vote rule a combination of members that lacked a majority of citizens could be the deciding factor in actions taken by the general government. If a larger than majority vote was used then a minority could always block the interests of the majority. The issue of a just representation for each member nation will also be a major consideration faced by the convention called to draft a constitution for a world government. Third, Hamilton points out that the general government did not contain an independent judiciary to act as the supreme arbitrator. When disputes arose the judiciary under the Articles could render a verdict but that verdict was in essence merely an advisory opinion.

In the modern world, all existing governments have been granted the powers necessary to repair the defects set forth above. They all are legally capable of independent financing, creating a military organization, enforcing their laws and regulations, controlling both internal and external commercial activities, and to resolve disputes on a final basis. All nations, however, have not created a system for conducting business in a way that insures equity for all their citizens; nor have they created an independent judiciary. The United Nations although created for purposes less extensive than that of a true government has none of these powers.

Hamilton's final conclusion is that the government created by the Articles of Confederation was so weak it could not be successfully reformed and by necessity should be scrapped. He admitted that the proposed constitution was not intended to reform the Articles but rather to create a whole new style of government.

In number 23 Hamilton presents the idea that he has reached the point where specific discussion of the proposed constitution could begin, i.e., he felt that the reasons for the type of government proposed by the new constitution had been explained and the defects of the old government sorted out. His conclusion was that the old government needed to be replaced by a government at least as strong as the one proposed. He presents his plan to break his discussion of specifics into three parts. First, the duties to be given to the general government under the proposed constitution will be discussed. Second, the amount of power that will be necessary to accomplish the responsibilities incorporated into the duties will be discussed. Third, the people who would be elected, or appointed, to exercise these powers will be discussed. The duties of the general government are set forth by Hamilton as follows.

> The principle purposes to be answered by union are these-the common defense of the members; the preservation of the public peace, as well against internal insurrection as external attacks; the regulation of commerce with other nations and between the states; the superintendence of our intercourse, political and commercial, with foreign countries.[1]

It is, of course, arguable that a general government of a world union would have both additional and different duties than those mentioned by Hamilton. It has been pointed out earlier, for example, that the world government would either have no duty, or very limited duties, in relation to the intercourse between

---

1 *The Federalist Papers*, No. 23, p. 85, Great Books of the Western World, Encyclopedia Britannica.

itself and non-member nations, both political and commercial. It might, however, have the additional duties of providing the means whereby environmental pollution would be stopped and cleaned up. It might have additional duties relating to the access and use of common areas, such as outer space, the open seas, and cyberspace. The powers enumerated by Hamilton, however, will be adequate to initiate debate upon the principle involved in any delegation of power to the general government.

In number 24 Hamilton presents the arguments for and against the maintenance of standing armies during times of peace. The arguments used are all contingent upon the circumstance of being one nation among many in the current system of nationalism. In our case the question is not whether standing armies are needed during times of peace, but rather, what level of professional military is necessary to guarantee the public peace. Specifically, this question would include that of whether or not a standing army is necessary, as well as the questions regarding the size of the military organization, the type of equipment it would need, and the limits on its use. For example, would the military only be used in cases involving violent insurrections, civil wars, or other disturbances of the public peace; or would it also be trained and used for disaster relief and general policing duties? In our case there can be no doubt that the first order of business in relation to the military will be total disarmament of all national military organizations, the destruction and safe disposal of all weapons of mass destruction, and the creation of an effective inspection system to guarantee compliance on the part of the member nations. The military force necessary to the general government upon completion of disarmament would be determined by the realistic appraisal of the threats then existing to the public peace, and any auxiliary duties that might be assigned to it. These threats would include, at least for some time, the threat of civil wars, policing duties in relation to acts of internal criminal activities, and short-term response to natural or manmade disasters. It would also include the long term duties that might be assigned in the area of reaction to disasters, either manmade or natural, such as toxic waste spills, changes in sea levels, hurricanes, tornadoes, and earth quakes. In the case of extraterritorial violence (acts of violence not associated with the insurrection involved), criminal activities, and invasions (such as those being waged in Afghanistan and Iraq), the military held by the general government would need only to be comparably equipped with those whom they fight. In the case of disaster relief they would need to be equipped appropriately for the duties they are expected to perform. In all likelihood in either case a force conventionally equipped with weapons and materials would be capable of executing their duties. Once the new system is in place the military maintained by the general government would be much smaller and much more economically equipped than even the current military of the US minus its weapons of mass destruction.

Many nations and peoples can be expected to resist giving up national sovereignty and regional rights to self-determination; or to view the establishment of world governance as a new form of colonialist exploitation. This would include groups that today are conducting local insurrections (and are seen by the US at least as terrorist activities); as well as those forces which operate outside of the political arena but which affect life within many nations (notably the operations of organized crime). It is also possible that the increasing demands of disaster relief may call for a larger civilian type military (similar to the existing National Guard in the U. S.). Handling these problems may require an initial force larger than what will be needed once these problems are brought under control. It is clearly understood that the solution to civil war, disaster relief, and criminal activity is essentially a political and economic one, but the force must be available to control violence from these sources until the other methods of resolution are put into effect. The total disarmament, the destruction and safe disposal of all weapons (especially weapons of mass destruction), and the disarming of resistance fighters and criminal activities, will add serious logistical problems. These same logistical problems are multiplied beyond calculation when left to the whims of two hundred sovereign governments each with specific interests in rejecting the attempt. The jealousy, the resistance, the damage to national pride, all point to a difficult resolution, as did the same issues in relation to the US Constitution. It is equally clear that only the strongest commitment on the part of the majority of nations, especially the most powerful nations, will be capable of bringing such projects to completion, as again was the case with the US Constitution (only on a much smaller scale).

In numbers 25 and 26, Hamilton extends his arguments concerning a standing army. The points he covers have been fully set forth in detail above and there is no need to reiterate them here.

In number 27, an attempt is made to handle the objection that the proposed government will be empowered to create so large a force (presumably military in nature, but not necessarily limited to military aspects) to enforce its laws that a danger of tyranny would arise. The answer provided by Hamilton is twofold. First, he claims that there is no reason to believe that the general government will be more poorly administered than any of the then existing states. The same fear could be raised in our case, that is, a justifiable fear of the size and power of the general government could raise fears of tyranny. To illustrate this point one must only keep in mind the maxim set forth by Alfred North Whitehead that 'power corrupts and absolute power corrupts absolutely'. If the history of the US can stand as a witness it would seem that the nations of the world have no more to fear from a general world government than the states had to fear from the federal government of the United States. Second, Hamilton points out that the laws of the general government would meet with no greater resistance, or need no more enforcement, than the laws of any particular state and in most cases probably even less. In our case the enforcement of the laws passed by the general legislature would be enforced by the existing policing institutions already in place in the several nations. In this instance one statement made by Hamilton deserves to be quoted here.

> I will, in this place, hazard an observation, which will not be less just because to some it may appear new; which is, that the more the operations of the national authority are intermingled in the ordinary exercise of government, the more the citizens are accustomed to meet with it in all common occurrences of their political life, the more it is familiarized to their spirit and to their feelings, the further it enters into those objects which touch the most active springs of the human heart, the greater will be the probability that it will conciliate the respect and attachment of the community.[1]

This has been proven to be an accurate assessment of the manner in which the federal government has operated in the US and it is expected that a world government based on that of the US would develop in a like manner. However, as pointed out by writers such as Francis Fukuyama this trust once earned can be abused by those who are in power in both the general government and in the state and local governments. It is possible that such an abuse of trust has a very profound effect upon the operation of a representative democracy.

Numbers 28 and 29 of the Papers deal with the issue of state militias as a means of guaranteeing a standing army for the use of the general government in case of external invasion or internal insurrection. In the United States today this militia is called the National Guard. In recent decades the National Guard has been used for disaster relief, such as with hurricanes and earthquakes within the boundaries of the US and lately in the military actions in Afghanistan and Iraq. The National Guard was originally a method under which young men and women could sign up for a designated number of years but remain at home and in gainful employment. Their training, and the officers for the Guard, was the responsibility of the several states. The National Guard was always subject to being called up to the regular military service, but, in fact, until the Afghanistan and Iraqi affairs they never had been on any significant level.

---

1 *The Federalist Papers*, No. 27, p. 95, Great Books of the Western World, Encyclopedia Britannica.

Since the declaration of war on Iraq, however, the US National Guard has been constantly on deployment with the regular armed services. In Hamilton's day, the militia was essentially guaranteed enough soldiers from the fact that nearly every man was armed and self-trained in the use of firearms. These men were capable of turning out for military service at a moment's notice.

One option that is available in our case is to forgo the establishment of a professional standing army under the control of the general government and allow each nation to continue to maintain a National Guard after the fashion of the current United States. This would be particularly important for quick deployment in the case of natural or manmade disaster relief. The National Guard would already be on location and the deployment would not require massive logistical support such as that which is needed when relief is dispatched from continents away. The National Guard would also be available to be called up for use as a standing army by the general government in case of serious internal insurrection, but again this would only be necessary if one of the National Guards, or several of them, were militarily involved in the insurrection.

It might also be necessary for the general government to be empowered to create and maintain a standing professional army if any significant number of nations decided not to join the union, at least, until all nations were totally disarmed. If the option of the National Guard is chosen without a standing army under the general governments control the power of the general government to activate the National Guard, or some part of them, must be absolute and not contributory as is the case with the current United Nations. In all military actions carried out under mandate by the United Nations a few wealthy populous nations have contributed the lion's share of the men, material, and financing particularly the United States. This even includes the financing of the day-to-day operation of the United Nations, let alone its military mandates. Even in such cases as the Korean "policing" action and the use of force in Afghanistan, the US alone has provided a majority of the men, materials, and financing.

There does not, therefore, seem to be any alternative to either delegating the power to the general government to create and maintain its own military organization; or to allowing the general government unrestrained access to the several National Guards. The same faith and credit must be given by the citizens that a world government would not make any unauthorized use of this force; just as the citizens of the early US extended such faith and credit to their new federal government. However, an argument can be made that large national forces are currently being used in opposition to the desire of the world's citizens. There is little doubt that opinion was solidly against the use of force in Iraq to overthrow the regime of Saddam Hussein. The US and Great Britain, however, led a small coalition of nations in an invasion of Iraq in defiance of world opinion. It is possible, therefore, to argue that military force can, and sometimes is, use in unauthorized circumstances even by governments based on representative democracy. However, the conscious use of the United Nations in relation to the action taken in Korea, in Kuwait, and in Afghanistan, all seems to argue that it is possible that world opinion, if aptly focused, can control the use of military force. On the other hand, the intentional distortion of military and civil intelligence by the United States and Great Britain to sway world opinion to favor the use of force in Iraq is a sign that the U.N. is ineffective if a major power decides to act.

Numbers 30, 31, 33 and 34 all written by Hamilton deal with the objections concerning the proposed taxation powers to be granted the federal government. The general arguments used, and at the time needed to answer the objections, have since 1790 all been conceded by modern liberal democracy, if not by all types of government. There is no question that the power of the general government to tax, either exclusively, or concurrently, is necessary to insure the independent ability to carry out the financing of day-to-day operations. In a representative republican democracy all levels of government, i.e., the state (in our case the National) governments, the city, village, town, township, county, etc., governments all have the power to tax their citizens. In the US, for example, the federal government has the right to establish all import and export taxes, to implement income taxes and other direct taxes. The state governments are also capable of assessing income taxes, gasoline taxes, licensing taxes, among others. While the cities, towns, townships, and county governments are capable of instituting real property taxes and sales taxes among others. Some such system will probably be established along with an effective world government. The problems that need to be avoided under such a taxation policy are the use of hidden taxes, the abuse of legal deductions from the taxes assessed, the fraudulent payment of taxes, or tax evasion totally, and others of a more specialized nature. The establishment of a world government offers an opportunity to reform all levels of taxation to provide for a just assessment of taxes in terms of payment and collection. Any issues that arise from the implementation, the enforcement, and the collection of taxes, at whatever level of government, must be capable of being settled by law in a timely manner. In a nutshell, the problems or areas of disagreement that will arise in the area of taxation are likely to be technical in nature rather than problems of general policy. It is likely that more concern will be needed to insure that the taxes granted do not create duplicate bureaucracies for the implementation, enforcement, and collection of taxes. A more detailed look at the taxing policies of the various governmental levels in the US will be needed by the proposed convention during the process of creating a constitution for a world government.

In numbers 35 and 36 Hamilton continues the discussion of taxation in a representative democracy. This question is not likely to be one of the most difficult problems to find a solution for, at least, from the practical point of view. The actual implementation of an equitable system of taxation on a worldwide scale is likely to be weighted down with practical problems. These problems will include, but probably not be limited to, a just system of insuring minority representation in the issue of which taxes are to be applied and by whom as well as a just means of insuring the exemption of religious organizations, if such an exemption is allowed, and the exemption of any other organizations that are deemed appropriate. Any exemptions that might be allowed on the level of individuals must be carefully scrutinized, and lastly, insuring that the total burden of taxation at all levels of government is equitably distributed between all the citizens subject to taxation.

The Federalist Papers set out a system that is based on the example of the powers of taxation granted by the proposed constitution. Hamilton expects that most taxes, with the exception of those given exclusively to the federal government, will be collected through the existing state tax institutions already in existence. Those that are exclusive in the federal government would probably require a separate bureaucracy such as the Internal Revenue Service (IRS) that exists in the United States. In relation to the general government Hamilton suggested that the knowledge of local tax systems, the condition of the revenue generated by them, and the sources of those taxes be made available to the federal government by the appropriate institution assigned the duty of collecting those taxes for the state or local governments. Hamilton suggested that the first congress should adopt this system even though it was not mandated by the constitution. As a matter of fact this tax system was adopted by the federal government shortly after its implementation.

In one area, however, the Federalist Papers presents a totally inaccurate viewpoint in regard to modern conditions. The Papers set forth the belief that the duties expected of the states would over time diminish, and that their need for revenue would be reduced in proportion to their loss of duties. While it is true that the states have voluntarily relinquished some of their original duties, and others have been legally absorbed by the federal government, their need for increased revenue has consistently grown throughout US history. In fact, today many of the state and local governments especially the large urban governments are on the brink of financial bankruptcy. This condition of need in terms of revenue on the part of state and local governments has required the infusion of huge sums of money by the federal government to insure the successful execution of the duties expected of the state and local governments. It cannot be predicted as to what types of problems will arise with the implementation of a world government. It may be that a much more detailed system of taxation will need to be created; one capable of on-going flexibility in terms of adjustment to the problems which do arise in relation to the national and local governments that continue to exist. It is unlikely that this type of problem can be profitably handled by a constitutional convention and the solution to them will need to be handled on a piece-meal basis by the various legislatures involved. In the US there are three areas that have contributed more than any others in producing the shortfall in revenue for the state and local governments.

First, it appears that the duty of the state and local governments in terms of the general welfare, that is, the provision for good schools, roads, bridges, sanitary and water systems, and police protection have far exceeded the ability of a relatively small territory and population to fund. Second, the same is true of the duty of state and local governments to provide for individual welfare, that is, unemployment, disability, and old age insurance, the providing of special programs for the disabled, insane, and incarcerated, as well as, providing aid for those subject to ill-health or poverty.

Currently it is becoming clear that not only states and local governments are incapable of funding such programs but that even the wealthiest of nations, such as the United States, Germany, and Japan are incapable of indefinitely maintaining the level of individual welfare they are providing. It is likely that the establishment of a world government will give the experts in these matters an opportunity to reform the current systems into a more effective method of providing for these needs. It may be that a designation of service will have to be made based on the length of time expected to be involved in the welfare offered. For example, it may be the duty of the general world government to implement only programs that are involved with long term illness, disability, or unemployment; while the state and local governments may only be responsible for the implementation of programs of a short term nature.

It may also be possible to self-fund some of the programs through pay-roll deductions as is currently done in the United States. However, to be effective this system must be restricted to the use intended and not allowed to become a part of the general fund of any level of government as is the case in the United States. It is currently unknown whether or not a program of individual welfare could be truly self-funding but it is, at least, possible that if proper safe guards were taken to insure the availability of the funds collected that they would be.

Third, the state and local governments have found themselves incapable of providing the manpower, materials, and financing needed to rapidly and effectively respond to major catastrophes. This is clearly evident when one looks at the response throughout the world to major catastrophes such as earthquakes, hurricanes, tornados, and floods. The quick and efficient response to such events is best achieved when directed from one central location, under the direction of one bureaucracy (department of government, or the military organization), and one source of financing.

The world government may be safely made responsible for the supervision of national organizations established just for the purpose of disaster relief. The national and local governments, however, must be made responsible for the rapid assessment of the needs generated by the disaster, and the materials and manpower necessary to resolve the needs. The national and local governments must also be responsible for the actual delivery of the disaster relief and for all follow up needed to fully resolve the problems created. The general government, in the end, would be responsible for funding the relief actually provided along with the materials and equipment necessary to resolve the issues.

Chapter 8. The Constitutional Convention and the General Powers Granted to the World Government

Numbers 38 and 39, written by James Madison, are intended as an introduction to a detailed look at the proposed constitution. In the process of introducing this task Madison raises a couple of issues that are of the first importance to our project. The first issue approached is how the convention, or other chosen method, for drafting the proposed constitution will be selected. Will it, for example, be selected by the chief executive officer of each nation that wishes to become a member? If not the chief executive officer, then will it be either the legislative branch, or a committee selected by the legislative branch? Second, once the method of selecting the candidates for the convention has been chosen, then it will be necessary to determine the number of candidates to be selected. In connection with the number of candidates to be selected it must also be determined if any qualifications are to be set forth as eligibility for the duty. The number of candidates should be determined by the maximum number that can be expected to efficiently carry on day-to-day business. If the number is too large the debate will be ceaseless and business will not be concluded. If the number is too small the likelihood that some nations will feel underrepresented will be great. The US Constitutional convention had fifty five representatives who were able to resolve all issues between them and then draft a proposed constitution in about four months. If care is taken in selecting the candidates, and a reasonable number of candidates can be chosen, there is no reason that the convention to write the proposed constitution for a world government could not accomplish the same task in a similar amount of time. Assuming, for the sake of argument, that every nation, by whatever method is chosen, selects two candidates to stand for election to the convention the total number available would be about four hundred. From this number a special committee chosen by the United Nations as a selection committee could consider the qualifications of each candidate and select one from each nation but no more than two hundred delegates. There does not seem to be any natural obstacle to the use of two hundred delegates, that is, the number does not seem to be excessive in relation to the effective operation of day-to-day business or issue resolution, nor does it seem excessive in relation to the drafting of a proposed constitution. One of the major benefits of this number is that each nation would be allowed one delegate to the convention. On the other hand, it has the detriment of allowing some collections of people (those not officially a part of a nation, or those who exist without the benefit of national citizenship) to be unrepresented in the convention. Third, assuming again that the delegates have been selected and that they have produced a proposed constitution, it will become necessary to determine a method whereby that constitution can be ratified. In the case of the US Constitution, it required that three fourths of the existing states (nine states) ratify the constitution before it could go into effect. The ratification was to be done either by the legislature of the various states, or by a convention selected by the legislature of each state. In our case two different methods could be used. The current method of adopting amendments to the U.N. Charter could be used to ratify the proposed constitution. The drawback to this method is that any one of five nations could block ratification regardless of how many nations desired to see it ratified. It would seem best to designate a certain percentage of nations needed to ratify the constitution before it go into effect, and to let the individual nations ratify the constitution, or reject it, by whatever method is in existence for such procedures in each nation. Lastly, once ratified a method must be determined to put the constitution into operation and to designate where and when the first general government is to meet.

It goes without saying that those chosen, in whatever number is decided upon, and in whatever manner chosen, be of such a caliber as to present the best possible chances for success. It is a certainty that one has to be in some degree of amazement that any group of people could produce a document such as the US Constitution with such speed and unanimity. Whether or not any other group of people could be found capable of producing a similar document, even with the benefit of having a model already available to them, remains to be seen. There were two major circumstances that seem the most important in the success of the US convention. First, those selected to sit in convention in 1789 were directly charged with creating a government of no other form than that of a republican representative democracy; and all the delegates chosen understood exactly what was intended in the charge given to them. They had all been involved in the drafting of the state constitutions, all of which were of the republican form, and had also been involved in the operation of these governments. Second, all the delegates had at hand the thirteen state constitutions to be used as models in drafting the proposed constitution. The state constitutions had been the result of an accumulation of experience at self-government stretching over a century and one half. In addition, the delegates had to a large degree firsthand knowledge of the failures incorporated into the operation of the government created by the Articles of Confederation. While the delegates chosen to the convention for drafting a constitution for a world government will not be qualified in just this way it is not unlikely that they will have very similar qualifications. It is hard to imagine a convention of delegates that would not have a very profound knowledge of the principles of republican representative democracy. If such a group were to be elected then the fault would not be with the delegates but with the selection process, or the process under which they were chosen as candidates by those who qualified them. This convention would also have the benefit of having the US Constitution as a model that has successfully operated for over two hundred years. It is also likely that the delegates would be familiar with the failings of organizations such as the United Nations and the European Union. That is to say the delegates would be familiar with the drawbacks that accompany organizations that operate as something less than a full government. It is also possible that a significant number of the delegates would have had extensive experience as members of either the United Nations, the European Union, or in the government of their respective nations. When compared to the delegates to the US Constitutional convention the differences expected tend to be minimized by like kind experience.

Secondly, Madison raises the question as to whether or not the convention should have been limited to reform of the Articles of Confederation. In addition, Madison considered the objection that the proposed constitution was not the best that could be created and therefore should be redone until the best document could be produced. There can be no doubt that Madison was correct when he pointed out that many of the articles that composed the constitution were arrived at after a considerable amount of compromise by all sides on the issues. There were compromises between the delegates of large states and small states, manufacturing interests and commercial interests, rural states and urban states, and others. There will also be equally important interests of the same nature, and many others, that the delegates to a constitutional convention for world government will face. The attitude towards compromise will need to be equally prevalent in the new convention as it was in the old. A few such interests would include large versus small nations, wealthy versus poor nations, nations wealthy in natural resources versus those without natural resources, nations predominant in the global market versus those who are not, Muslim versus non-Muslim nations, etc., etc. It is just these types of issues that will be in need of the spirit of compromise not to mention the issues of environment pollution, total disarmament, and the equitable distribution of natural resources, and their conservation, which seem today totally insoluble. Therefore, Madison was wise to preface the Federalist discussion of the actual articles of the proposed constitution with the outstanding characteristics of those who served in the convention. He was equally wise in pointing out that a compromise was needed to obtain agreement on nearly every article of the constitution, which at that time consisted of eight articles. The conclusion drawn by Madison was that the best that could be chosen to serve in the convention had actually been chosen, and the best document that could be produced, when consideration was given to the degree of compromise needed, was in fact produced. The decision, therefore, was only whether or not this particular document should be accepted, or rejected, based on its own merits alone. The same arguments should be considered if a convention is called, and a constitution drafted, for the institution of a world government.

In numbers 38 and 39 Madison begins the discussion of the actual form of government created by the proposed constitution. First, he considers whether or not the new government would qualify as a representative democracy. Secondly, he looks into the determination of whether the new government would be a federal or national government in character. He begins by defining the rules by which a representative democracy can be determined. If it is a representative democracy then all of the power resides ultimately in the people. As far as practicable, according to Madison, this is what has occurred in the proposed constitution, that is, all the powers that have been delegated to the general government, or denied to the state governments, or yet reserved to the people, are in fact all the powers available to any form of government. Madison next considers whether the proposed constitution would be federal or national in character. If national all of its powers would be directly applicable to all of the citizens of the union, and whatever powers were retained by the states would be those specifically delegated by the general government. If strictly federal all of the powers of the general government would only be applicable to the states in their corporate capacity as independently sovereign governments. Madison concludes that the proposed constitution creates a hybrid government, that is, a government that is federal in its foundation, i.e., one that will be ratified by the operation of the states as independently sovereign governments. In the sources of its ordinary powers, however, Madison asserts that the general government is both federal and national, i.e., that some of its powers apply to the states only in their corporate capacity, and other of its powers apply directly to the citizens of the union. In actual operation Madison believes the new government is intended to be national in character as all its laws are to be applied directly to the citizens rather than to the states alone. In the extent of the power of the general government, however, the intent was federal in nature in the sense that the powers that were given to the general government were limited in nature. A large degree of its power is to be shared with the several states in their corporate capacity. In the case of amendments to the constitution the intent is again federal as amendments can be initiated either by the federal congress or a set percentage of the state legislatures. The proposed constitution offered above was written using the US Constitution as a model. When looked at with the definitions used by Madison it is equally national and federal in construction. The failures of purely federal governments are confirmed throughout history; and the success of national governments is no guarantee that such a government would succeed on the worldwide level. Over the last one hundred years, especially the seventy years since the great world wars, the use of republican representative democracy, which in essence is a mixture of federalism and nationalism has been most widely accepted. As a result it appears to such men as Francis Fukuyama that the world has slowly adopted the opinion that republican representative democracy is the most viable form of government available to the several nation-states. As stated earlier, it may be necessary to rearrange the relative importance of the federal and national character incorporated into the world government. This decision will, of course, be based upon the issues that face the convention in its task of drafting the initial constitution.

In number 40 Madison attempts to determine whether or not the convention exceeded the powers granted to it by the states when they approved the convention. It is not really necessary for us to look in detail at this issue. Any convention called to draft a proposed constitution for a world government would not be in any way limited to a reform of the U.N. charter, as this charter was never intended to create a world government in the manner intended by the creation of the Articles of Confederation. In short, any convention called to draft a constitution for the implementation of a world government should be understood to have the power to create any document, no matter how radical, in successful completion of this task. Under this type of charge it should be clear that the convention is not limited to reforming the U.N. charter, or to recreating the United States in the form of a world government. In our case, if the charge is given to create a proposed constitution, regardless of the method chosen to call the convention, or to select the delegates, the authorization given the convention should be as broad as possible. The convention should be charged with producing a document intended solely to create a republican representative democracy capable of effectively governing a union of up to two hundred nations. It should also be understood that any document produced by the convention will stand only as advice and recommendation to the existing nations who will debate its merits concerning acceptance or rejection. However, should the requisite number of nations ratify the document the document then would become the supreme law of the union formed by it. It should again be pointed out that with this constitution, as with the constitution of the US, a few key nations must ratify it before it can have any hope of success.

In number 41 Madison begins the attempt to explain the actual powers granted to the general government under the constitution. He breaks these powers into six classes. First, the power to protect the proposed union from external attack and internal insurrection; second, the power to regulate all intercourse with foreign nations; third, the power to preserve the harmony and proper intercourse among the states; fourth, the power to institute certain objects of general utility; fifth, the power to restrain the states from certain injurious acts; lastly, the intention to put into effect all the above powers.

Those powers falling under the first class include the power to declare war and peace; the power to call forth the state militia; and the levying and borrowing of money to pay for the use of the military in problem resolution. Madison seems to be correct in his assessment that the power to declare war must reside with someone, especially when one's view is restricted to the existing system of nationalism that existed in 1790.

The same is true, in light of nationalism, in regard to the powers creating and maintaining a standing professional military, the equipping of such a military institution, and in the direction of such a military in times of shooting war. Madison's conclusion is that the most efficient, and least dangerous, place to put these powers is with the general government. The two hundred year history of the US appears to confirm his conclusion. These considerations, however, only apply when one is considering the existing system of nationalism. However, the history of the US offers some support for the conclusions drawn by Madison. In the conduct of foreign campaigns that have been entered into by the United States it is at least arguable that no more efficient conduct of war has been evidenced by any other system of command.

The same seems to be true of the control over whatever internal insurrection that has occurred. The sole exception appears to be the US civil war, which was fought between 1860 and 1865. It should be noted, however, that in this case the term civil war is somewhat misleading. Eleven states attempted to exercise what they considered to be their legal right to voluntarily withdraw from the union.

There was nothing in the Constitution, or in the laws that had been passed by the federal legislature, which made it specifically illegal to withdraw from the union. In fact, it is possible to show from the source documents that the creators of the Constitution considered that the right to end the union, if they saw fit, was reserved to the states. It was not, however, specifically written into the Constitution nor had it been specifically ruled upon by the Supreme Court. The legislatures of the eleven states involved each passed a law withdrawing them from the union, that is, they proceeded as if their objective was allowed under the Constitution. It is possible to see their action as a test of the legality of voluntary withdrawal from the union.

One has to wonder what would have happened if the remaining members of the union had taken the opportunity to test the validity of the action in the Supreme Court. If legal action had been taken and the Supreme Court had ruled that the eleven states had taken legislative action that was unconstitutional, and the eleven states had continued in their actions of withdrawal from the union, then the actions would clearly fit the definition of rebellion or internal insurrection. That was not the course taken, and the remaining members of the union immediately opted for the use of military force to resolve the issue.

In any definition of civil war it is understood that both sides in the contest are contending for the right to exercise political control over the whole nation or whatever subdivision is under contention. The US civil war was in all essentials a case where one side was contending for the right to control its own destiny and the other side was attempting to force the continuation of the union. If the eleven states that had voluntarily withdrawn from their adherence to the union had won the war, it is certain that two independent nations would have been the result.

It is very important that this distinction is understood, as any withdrawal from the world union in our case would be exactly the same as the withdrawal of the eleven states from the early United States. This, however, is not the place to take a more detailed look at the consequences that arose from the initiation of the US civil war and its conclusion. It seems apparent that the issue of voluntary withdrawal from a voluntary union has yet to be definitively decided. In response, the constitution of the world government might incorporate a provision outlawing the voluntary dissolution of the union after acceptance by any nation, or group of nations, except in the case of unanimous agreement to dissolve the union.

The general government, however, must have the power to prevent violent insurrections that amount to something less than dissolution of the union. In short, the general government must be capable to resolving all disputes between its members or any other situation capable of expanding into violence upon request or necessity. In addition, the general government must be authorized to act in any case of natural or manmade disaster, requiring relief beyond the capability of any specific national government. The same would be true, at least initially, in response to the repression of international crime and random acts of insurrection.

In number 42 Madison takes up the issue of the powers of the second class. These powers are only applicable when one is analyzing the system of nationalism now in place. Some nations that currently exist may opt to not join the world union. It is also possible that new nations will be created after the world union has been initiated and they may decide not to join. In either case there will be a need for the general government to have the power to control relations between the union and these nations. Under the US Constitution the power to make treaties, or other contracts, to send and receive ambassadors, consuls, and other foreign dignitaries was granted solely to the federal government and denied specifically to the states. These powers would have to be adjusted to fit the circumstances that existed at the time that the world union was put into operation. If all existing nations initially joined the union the types of powers set forth would not be necessary. If one or more nations did not join the union then they would need to be focused on a method of interacting with these nations or societies. In the former case the powers needed by the general government would revolve around the common areas that remained after the union was initiated, that is, outer space, the open seas, unincorporated land masses, and cyberspace. It would be necessary to delegate the power to regulate these areas, and to act with finality in all disputes that might arise involving them, solely to the general government. These areas would include the continent of Antarctica and the Arctic. In short, the general government would still need to be empowered to pass all laws, edicts, and regulations concerning the access and use of these common areas, as well as, the power to enforce them if necessary.

Madison also approaches the issues arising from the third class of powers. These powers, according to Madison, are intended to promote (enforce) harmony and proper intercourse between the member states. They include the power to regulate commerce between the states (interstate commerce); to coin money; to regulate the value of money; to provide for the punishment of the crime of counterfeiting the securities or money of the union. They also include the power to fix a uniform standard of weights and measures; to provide for uniform rules of naturalization; to provide uniform rules for filing and obtaining bankruptcy relief. They also include the power to proscribe how the public acts, records, and judicial proceedings of the several states shall be proven, and the effect they will have in the other states. The third class of powers also gave the general government the power to create and maintain a uniform postal service throughout the union, including the duty to provide adequate post roads. In connection with the establishment of an effective world government it is imperative that the general government have the sole power to regulate trade between the member nations and between the member nations and any nations that might remain outside the union. The general government should also be granted the sole power to create a uniform monetary system, to regulate the value of that system, to create a uniform system of weights and measures, to establish and operate a uniform postal service, and the punishment of counterfeiting. The general government should also have the sole power of determining the conditions that would allow application for bankruptcy and the effect of the relief that granting of bankruptcy would allow. The power to establish the rules for naturalization would not be needed if all nations joined the union, but would need to be in place should one, or more, nations not join, or if any society of people composing something less than a nation remained outside the union. The general government would, however, be required to establish the method by which the laws of one state could be proven in another state and the effects of that proof. In the case of weights and measures it is recommended that the metric system be used as it currently has the widest use. It is also recommended that the European Union be used as a model for the construction and valuation of a uniform monetary system, maybe even using the Euro as the standard for the new system. The European Union has apparently been successful in creating a uniform monetary system where before there existed many separate monetary systems. The methods used by the European Union to determine the conversion rates for the old currencies, as well as the initial evaluation of the new currency would be invaluable. Lastly, upon the initiation of the world union all the people who accepted the union would automatically become citizens of both the world union and nation in which they resided. They would automatically be entitled to give and receive the full faith and credit of each other's laws, records, and judicial proceedings. The United States and the European Union both stand as excellent examples of how best to incorporate dual citizenship into the day-to-day lives of the people that are affected. The European Union is a good example of how the other powers mentioned above would operate in the case of a world government.

In number 43 Madison approaches the powers of the fourth class. These include the following powers: one, the power to grant protection to artists and inventors through the issuing of limited copyrights and patents. Two, the general government would be delegated the power to make all laws, edicts and regulations necessary to maintain land, or other property, dedicated to its use. This power would apply whether that land or property is within the area designated as the common capitol, or within the boundaries of a particular state. Such property would include arsenals, government buildings, business personal property, etc. Three, the general government would have the power to define and punish the crime of treason. Four, the general government would have the power to define the rules under which a new state might be admitted to the union; and to provide the rules under which a new state might be created from a part of an existing state, or parts of two or more states. Five, the general government would be delegated the power to guarantee the peaceful enjoyment of a republican form of government to the individual states. Six, the general government would have the power to extinguish the debts incurred and still outstanding under the Articles of Confederation. In the situation of a world union the powers found in one, two, three and four would remain essentially unchanged in import. The power conferred in five would probably undergo some change both in content and import. It can be reasonably expected that some nations, maybe a significant number of nations, will join the union without the benefit of a republican form of democracy as their national government. For example, it is likely that the nations with exclusive Muslim populations, or even large majority Muslim populations, will want to establish some form of theocracy. Whatever form of government is in place when a nation comes into the union that form of government will be guaranteed in regard to peaceful enjoyment and continuation by the general government. There does not seem to be any particular reason why the union would be unsuccessful merely because all members did not have a local democratic government. They would still be under the obligation to accept the constitution, to enforce the laws of the union, and give full, faith, and credit to the laws of all nations. It may be that over time the current trend towards liberal democracy will continue until all nations do in fact have a democratic form of national government, but until then it is necessary that a free determination of the form of government be allowed to each nation and its citizens. Under power six the world union would be responsible for the debts and other outstanding expenses of the United Nations and other international organizations such as the World Bank.

As an aside, it can be expected that the convention will set forth the rules under which the constitution can be ratified and a rule determining when it will go into effect. This set of rules might be classified as the seventh division of powers set forth above. If all nations are to be included in the proposed union then it is recommended that the constitution go into effect after three fourths of the nations have ratified it. If, however, a significant number of nations are not to be included in the initial union then it is recommended that a two-thirds rule be used to determine when the constitution would go into effect. Madison, at this point, raises two very interesting questions. First, he asks what standard, if any, should be established to allow one, or a combination of nations, to dissolve their membership in the union once it is established. Madison's answer to this question revolves around the understanding of the law concerning treaties and other contracts. In the case of treaties and contracts, according to Madison, it was understood that when one party breached any portion of the treaty or contract the other parties could at will consider the treaty or contract dissolved. In the case of a legislative ratification nothing more than what is expected in a contract or treaty could be expected. In short, Madison wants a unanimous affirmation of all members to dissolve the union, but accepts the wisdom of his day that the members could voluntarily withdraw their membership. In the case of the world union it is suggested that it be written into the constitution that after acceptance only a unanimous vote would dissolve the union. Second, what relation is to exist between those states that join the union (in this case it would have to be a minimum of nine states) and those states who decided to remain outside the union? Madison's answer is the only one available, i.e., the relations would be the same as those that now exist between independent sovereign nations. The same would be true in the case of a world union that did not contain all existing nations. Once again it is understood that the decision of any one or combination of key nations to remain outside the union greatly limits the possibility for success of the union. The same was true in the case of the US union that is, without key states like New York the hope of success for the union was limited, hence the motivation for publishing the Federalist Papers.

In number 44, Madison addresses the fifth class of powers. In Madison's view these powers took the form of prohibitions against specified actions by the individual states. The prohibitions include the following: one, the states were prohibited from making any treaties, alliances, or confederations with any member state, or group of states, or any foreign nation. Two, the states were prohibited from granting any letters of marquee and reprisal. In short, they could not offer any reward for the capture and delivery of any person or any property. Three, the states were prohibited from creating any local monetary systems or system of credit. They were, in other words, required to submit to the national monetary standard and national credit system. Four, the states were prohibited from making anything but gold and silver (at the time the exclusive method of setting the value of any monetary system) legal tender for the payment of debt. Five, the states were prohibited from issuing any ex post facto laws, any bills of attainder, or any laws impairing the obligations of contract. This latter power has been of great consequence in the historical development of the US especially in relation to the obligations of corporate operations. The prohibitions that are included in the above list are matters of common sense when one takes into consideration that the goal is to establish an effective general government. It is again suggested that the European Union may provide a very useful guide as to what should, or should not, be prohibited to the several nations under a world union.

In this same number Madison moves on to consider the powers contained in the sixth class. In regard to this class of powers, nothing more need be said than that it is impossible for an effective government to be instituted if it does not have the power to make the laws, edicts, and regulations necessary to implement its powers. In the same regard, if a republic is created, the laws of the general government must be understood to be the supreme law of the union, regardless of what may be contained in the constitutions, laws, edicts, regulations, or religious tenets of any member nation. In our case the most difficult hurdle may be found in the situation in which any particular law of the union is contrary to a specific religious tenet. It can only be expected in this case that each individual will be capable of separating his secular and religious duties. As in most legal systems that exist today there are always specific case by case exceptions that can be made in matters of true conscience. Lastly, the executive, legislative, and judicial branches of each nation must be charged with the duty of enforcing any valid law passed by the general government, and ruled constitutional by the Supreme Court. The latter, of course, includes the right of any nation and every citizen to challenge the constitutionality of any law passed by the general government, national government, or any local subdivision of government through the proper peaceful legal channels.

In numbers 45 and 46 Madison examines the objections put forward to the new constitution claiming that if put into effect it would soon denude the individual states of their remaining powers. The arguments presented by Madison on this question consisted of generalities as there was no historical precedent from which to draw specific examples. Madison has shown in the previous numbers, at least to his satisfaction, that the powers that had been granted to the general government were neither excessive nor dangerous, but rather, were only those necessary to allow the government to be effective. The general arguments began with the observation that the sovereignty of the federal government was so limited that the balance of power would almost certainly remain with the states. The general arguments concluded with the observation that the powers of the general government may be found to be inadequate to the task intended for it. In our case we do have the historical precedents that allow for us to argue from specific example. First, historical precedent has shown that Madison's prediction that the balance of power would slowly swing to favor the states was wrong. Over time the federal government's power has increased dramatically in comparison to that of the individual states, or in comparison with the states as a whole. Some of this power increase has resulted from the intervention of the federal government into areas that had been intended to be handled by the states originally. In some cases the states voluntarily abandoned the power as beyond their ability to execute, and in other cases the federal government usurped them through legal channels, or through legislative initiative or executive order. This shift in the power balance began at the very beginning and was driven by the Federalist Party. The philosophical position of this party was that the federal government should be as powerful as possible. The opposite position was taken by the Republican-Democratic party whose philosophy called for the limitation of the federal government and the strengthening of the state governments. As it turned out, however, for the first twelve years the executive department was held by the Federalists and the legislative branch was composed of a small majority of Federalists. When John Adams, a Federalist, left office he "packed" the federal judicial system with federalists, including the chief justice of the Supreme Court John Marshall. The judicial system remained solidly federalist in philosophical orientation until about 1834, or for another thirty three years. For the next eight years the Republican-Democrats held the executive branch and a small majority in the legislature. During these eight years the Federalist Party slowly dissolved, but the federalist philosophy was taken up by the new party that arose to replace it. The early Supreme Court decisions were the most important aspect of this ideological battle. Although the federal government obtained no new powers through this means, the powers that it had been granted were interpreted in such a way as to make it possible to extend their use into areas not intended by the original constitution. Second, it was discovered early in US history that the states and their local subdivisions were not capable of independently funding the projects needed to insure the general welfare of their citizens. The states, and the local subdivisions of government, were expected to provide the infrastructure needed to provide for the welfare of the citizens, such as roads, canals, bridges, schools, etc., the only exception being the constitutional duty of the general government to provide post roads. The states, in combination with the use of private capital, had taken the early lead in providing for the construction and maintenance of these facilities. By 1820, however, the construction of interstate canals and railway systems brought to light the impracticality of state funded projects of this type. Both these types of infrastructure were meant to service commercial needs rather than the needs of private citizens. They were distinctly intended to promote trade between the various states, that is, they were intended to be interstate in nature. The cost of constructing the canals and the railways, although initially handled almost exclusively through state and private funds, soon became far too costly to be funded solely by state and private means. The federal government was finally forced to step in under its power to regulate interstate commerce and provide the funding necessary. As the union began to rapidly expand into the Tennessee and Ohio River valleys the expectation arose that the federal government should take the responsibility for planning, funding, and regulating the construction of these interstate projects. The infrastructure needs of the country still remain under a concurrent power structure, but the majority of the funding and regulation is handled by the federal government. There appears to be a need for a detailed look at the consequences of this absorption of power by the federal government on the underlying principles of republican democracy. It is of particular interest in relation to the powers that have devolved on the federal government by means of the attachment of riders to the appropriation bills needed for funding state and local projects. It appears that in many cases these attachments had little, or nothing, to do with the project itself. For example, a few years ago a cry went up from the public concerning the number of deaths that were occurring on interstate highways. By attaching riders to the appropriation bills for the funding of the states portion of the interstate highway, either construction, or maintenance, it was possible for the federal government to force the states to accept a fifty five mile an hour speed limit across the board. Later the same scenario would be played in the failure of state and local governments, and the private charitable organizations, to cope with the growing problem of individual welfare needs, such as unemployment, disability, old age, health concerns, etc. Most recently the same has occurred in the area of disaster relief, such as the relief needed to cope with the Hurricane damage in New Orleans. These latter problems have not only been found in the inability of state and local governments, as well as, private charitable organizations in the US but also in the ability of national governments to fund them. The proposed constitutional convention should take a detailed look at the effect that federal government takeover of these types of projects has had on republican democracy.

The same issues that have faced the US during its historical evolution will be faced by a world union but on even larger scales. The inability of many nations to provide even a basic standard of living for its citizens, coupled with the inability, in many cases, of preventing fraud and abuse of any efforts put forth to solve these problems will have to be addressed by the world government. In fact, if recent history is any guide, one of the major problems that will face the world government will be the creation of an effective system to prevent fraud, shoddy workmanship, and waste of funds on whatever projects it decides to fund. A real assessment of the current systems in place around the world to prevent such practices will need to be made and the necessary repairs to make them effective will need to be made. In relation to the last statement it will probably be necessary to strictly define the responsibilities of the various levels of government in regard to their part in the planning, implementation, and execution of such projects; and the accounting necessary to insure efficient use of the funds available. It will also be necessary to look in detail at the type of services to be provided in the area of individual welfare and the cost of providing that service over extended periods of time. It may even be necessary to periodically adjust the definition of what constitutes a minimum standard of living. It will also be necessary in this area to determine the exact role to be played by each level of government, and any private secular organizations that care to participate, and how they will operate within the total system. In the end the accounting system used will need to be foolproof in tracking the expenditure of every public dollar. For example, it may be that the general government may be largely responsible for establishing the overall planning involving the type of programs that will be available for individual welfare and for the funding of such programs. The national governments, and their local subdivisions, may be responsible for qualifying those who apply for the program and for the actual payment of funds to be distributed by the program. This may include creating the systems necessary to prevent fraud and abuse and for creating the systems for following up on the continued individual need for assistance. Lastly, the general government may be responsible for establishing the independent accounting of the funds actually expended within the programs. What has to be kept in mind is that the overall planning and supervision (direction) of such programs is most effectively done by as concentrated generalship as possible therefore, at the highest level. While all the practical tasks of determining actual need, the cost of these needs, and the distribution and protection of the funds distributed is best handled at the lowest possible level, that is, the level that is most closely involved in the problems. The fiasco created by the federal handling of all levels of relief given after Hurricane Katrina is a good example to point.

There are, of course, some problems that cannot be solved by leaving the solutions in the hands of the individual nations. Such problems include the process of total disarmament, with the needed systems of verification, destruction, and safe disposal of waste from it; the conservation of the world's natural resources; the prevention and clean up of environmental pollution; and the effective policing and regulation of the common areas such as the open seas, outer space and cyberspace. Even here, however, it is to be expected that the general planning, funding, and supervision of these projects will fall to the general government, while the actual implementation and execution of them will fall to the national and local governments.

It must be kept in mind that the creation of a world union, whether based upon liberal democratic principles, or some other form of government, does not imply any type of balance of power between the general government and the national governments. It may not even be possible to list the powers that would be necessary for each level of government to obtain such a balance. The balance, whatever it may be, will over time arise from the necessary distribution of powers to rationally solve the problems that arise. It may be necessary from time to time to either limit or expand the power held by one or another of the two levels of government to effectively solve specific problems. It is for this reason that the constitution that initiates a world government must remain as general, flexible, and capable of reinterpretation from time to time as possible. The US Constitution, over its history, has remained a general document having been officially altered only twenty seven times and has been capable of reinterpretation by the Supreme Court when necessary to solve unforeseen problems. In this sense it has shown itself to be an extremely flexible document. In the end it appears likely that the current faith in the system of nationalism; as well as, the currently expressed desire of the world's people to maintain cultural diversity, will stand as the major obstacles to the implementation of an effective world union. Obstacles such as these are of the type that are not, in any meaningful sense of the word, overcome, but rather, are of the type that require they be accepted and incorporated into the underlying principles that form the basis of the world union. There does not seem to be any inherent defect in the principles which underlay liberal democracy that would require the dismantling of the existing nation states, or the homogenization of the diverse cultures that now exist. It seems likely that they can, and should, be allowed to evolve within the union as part of the process or evolution of the union as a unit.

Chapter 9. The Constitution, Branches of Government, and the Articles

The authors of the Federalist Papers have now concluded the general considerations that support the creation of the United States, and the constitution that will create it; especially the powers that they feel can safely be delegated to the federal government, and denied to the several states. They now turn their attention to an analysis of the wording of each article of the constitution.

In numbers 47 and 48 Madison presents the question of whether the three proposed branches of government, i.e., the executive, legislative, and judicial, should be independent of one another; or whether, each branch should have some type of supervisory power over the others. While it is instructive to read the arguments given by Madison, in particular, if one is attempting to determine the intention of those who framed the constitution they in the end are not relevant to modern conditions. Today mainly from the experience garnered from US history it is understood that in a representative democracy the three branches of government are going to be both independent and have supervisory powers over the others. The US Constitution, as well as the one proposed here, both create three independent branches of government. They also give each branch checks and balances to allow supervisory power to be exercised between them. Not all democratic systems have as bold a separation of the government functions as that found in the United States. For example, in the Parliamentary system of Great Britain the executive and judicial functions of government are closely intertwined with the legislative function. In fact, it is fair to say that only the House of Commons can be designated as a representative body. The executive leaders, as well as the judicial personnel, are appointed by the legislative branch, that is, the House of Commons. The executive branch serves only as long as it can retain its majority coalition of parties in the House of Commons, which is periodically determined by a vote of confidence in that House.

As mentioned above the mixed system found in the US became known as the system of checks and balances. The powers delegated to one branch of government were checked and balanced against those delegated to the other two branches. For example, the executive branch was given the sole right to conduct negotiations and to secure treaties with foreign nations. This power, however, was subject to the advice and consent of the Senate, that is, the treaty would not go into effect unless it was approved by a two-thirds vote of the Senators then in session. The same was true of the power of appointment given to the executive branch. The executive had the power to appoint all officers of the government as well as all federal judges. These appointments were again subject to the approval of the senate. While the legislative branch could not force the executive to choose any particular candidate they could force him to choose until he hit on one satisfactory to them. On the other hand, the legislature was given the sole power to pass laws. This power, however, was subject to the veto of the executive and to being ruled unconstitutional by the Supreme Court. The executive veto could be overcome by a more inclusive vote of both houses of the legislature, but the ruling of unconstitutionality by the Supreme Court could not be repaired. The people, however, hold the final check on power in both the executive and legislative branches in their hands. They, through the use of the periodic ballot, can peacefully replace both the executive and legislative leaders. The judiciary, however, is immune to even this check as they are appointed essentially for life (they serve a term bounded only by good behavior and death).

In our case the US Constitution is offered in a somewhat adapted format as the constitution that will create a world government. Under this constitution the same system of checks and balances has been incorporated. The three branches would be created separately, each would be delegated specific duties and responsibilities, and each would have supervisory powers over the others. The overall experience of the US has been that no branch of government, or combination of branches, has been able to usurp the powers of any other branch. The various checks and balances, coupled with the actual rules and regulations for the operation of each branch has at times created problems with the efficient handling of problems; but this may be one of the prices that must be paid to insure that the ultimate source of all power remains with the people. Indeed, it is probably safe to say that the three branches of government must have some degree of independence, while at the same time being subject to restrictions which prevent the power of all three collecting in one branch only. This was a major concern with those who objected to the US Constitution. Hamilton's answer was that the system created by the constitution was the only guarantee, if a guarantee it was, that could be made assuring the ultimate source of power remain with the people. He also concluded that the only way to safely delegate these powers was through the use of a representative democracy.

Numbers 49, 50, and 51 were written by either Madison, or Hamilton, and are intended to extend the arguments concerning the safeguards written into the constitution as checks and balances. From the benefit of experience with the use of checks and balances it is felt that no further examples beyond those given above are needed to establish this point. Each check and balance is set forth in the constitution itself and is left for the reader to peruse at his or her leisure.

Numbers 52 and 53 examine the constitutional provisions concerning the proposed House of Representatives. It is worth a direct quote to establish the thoughts behind the argument concerning the House of Representatives (in the convention debate) and the objections that were raised to it.

> A representative of the United States must be of the age of twenty-five years; must have been seven years a citizen of the United States; must, at the time of his election, be an inhabitant of the state he is to represent; and, during the time of his service, must be in no office under the United States. Under these reasonable limitations, the door of this part of the federal government is open to merit of every description, whether native or adoptive, whether young or old, and without regard to poverty or wealth, or to any particular profession of religious faith.[1]

> With the sole exception of the seven year citizenship requirement the same limitations would apply to those who would serve as representatives in the House of Representatives of the United Nations of Earth. The House of Representatives was obviously intended to be the part of the federal government open to all of the people. Initially it was the only federal institution subject to the direct vote of the people. In this it appears that the example found in Great Britain was copied in that the House of Commons was the only part of the parliamentary system subject to the direct ballot of the people. It was expected that this part of the federal government would maintain the closest and most open communication with the people. The argument presented that the use of frequent elections, in this case biannual elections, were needed to sustain this close contact with the people. A detailed look at whether or not the intended close contact of the Representatives with their constituents has been maintained in the US system will need to be undertaken as this will be one of the major concerns of the proposed convention. One objection raised was that the frequency of elections made it unlikely that those who served would have the requisite experience and knowledge to do a competent job. The

---

1 *The Federalist Papers*, No. 52, p. 165, Great Books of the Western World, Encyclopedia Britannica.

Federalist concedes that anything less than two years would in fact tend to leave those who served with inadequate knowledge to fulfill their task. The Federalist also extended the argument that the people would reelect those who they perceived to have done an adequate job. In fact, they could be reelected to as many two year terms as the people saw fit to allow them to have. Over time many of the representatives would become very experienced and knowledgeable concerning what was expected of them. Both the histories of the US and Great Britain clearly indicate that the term of office, in our case two years, is adequate to allow the Representatives to do their job at a considerable level of competence. It appears that history has confirmed that it is much more important that incompetent, or corrupt, representatives be capable of being ejected by the people quickly, that is, after a short period of time. The people have shown themselves eminently capable of collectively making a valid judgment concerning the character and competence of their representatives.

In Numbers 54 and 55, the writers take into consideration the number of representatives that will make up the proposed House of Representatives. The Papers indicate that at the time three main objections had been raised concerning the proposed number of representatives. First, it was objected that the number would be too small a number to be a safe depository for the powers that were to be delegated to them. Second, that the representatives would not possess a proper knowledge of their constituents interests. Third, the objection was raised that the representatives would all be from the same class of society. Initially upon acceptance of the constitution the number of representatives had been arbitrarily set at sixty five. It was expected, however, that after fifty years of operation the House of Representatives, using the designated census method of determining the total number, would result in there being over four hundred members. Today the US House of Representatives contain five hundred and thirty five members. In our case there is only one question that must be faced and that is how to limit the number of representatives to a number that will allow an efficient conduct of business, and yet, be a fair system of representation for all member nations. The problem of size evolves from the effort to avoid the problems that arise under the so-called "mob" syndrome. The question involves the determination of the number, in terms of a definite range of people, who are given a specific task to complete and who will be able to efficiently accomplish that task. The House of Representatives, for example, is expected to efficiently propose, debate, and pass all legislation dealing with the appropriation and expenditure of public funds. This would, of course, include the expectation that such legislation would be timely, clear in intent, and clear in scope. It would also be expected that the House would produce legislation that is capable of being enforced and that they will be capable of maintaining oversight of the required actions incorporated in the legislation. The problem is to determine when the number of people selected to fulfill this task will be either too small to effectively handle the amount of work expected of them, or too large to be able to conduct business at all. We can begin with the fact that the US House of Representatives has five hundred and thirty five members and seems to be capable of efficiently and effectively handling the business assigned to it, although it does not always do so. If the current system for determining the number of representatives in the US House is used the number of representatives in the House attached to a world government would be around two hundred thousand. I think it is safe to say that such a vast number of people would be totally unable to conduct business in any manner. Currently in the US each state is allowed one representative for every thirty thousand citizens. The number of two hundred thousand can be reduced in two ways; first, the nations could be allowed one representative for every twenty five million citizens, with the caveat that each nation would be allowed at least one representative. Under this system the number of representatives would be reduced to about two hundred members. Second, the number of representatives could be based upon an arbitrary number, i.e., each nation would be allowed a quota of representatives with the largest nations getting no more than twenty five and the smallest no less than one. This would currently result in about one thousand three hundred and fifty representatives. It is unknown whether this number would be unmanageable or not in relation to effective action. Whatever method is finally chosen to determine the number of representatives to be allowed each nation it must satisfy two requirements, that is, it must be equitable in terms of representation per nation and it must result in a body capable of conducting its business in an efficient manner. One problem that would need to be addressed, if population is to be used as the determining factor, is the question of China and India. Together these two nations represent about one third of the world's population and would, therefore, have over one third of the representatives in the House. This would allow for the possibility that they, in conjunction with a small number of other nations, could maintain a majority voice in the House. It is suggested that the only effective method would be to assign a definite number of representatives to each nation with a minimum and maximum number of representatives being determined. It would still be true that China and India would have the greatest number of representatives, but with such a great number of nations involved, no two nations, or even a small number of nations, would be able to garner a majority vote in the House. If a smaller number of representatives are desired then the only requirement would be to lower the maximum number of representatives allowable.

Another system that might be used that has nothing at all to do with population would be a districting system. For example, all nations could be divided into districts, with five districts being the maximum allowable to any one nation, and every nation consisting of, at least, one district. This would result in a House of Representatives with between five and eight hundred members. If a smaller number was desired then the only requirement would be to lower the maximum number of districts allowable. This system might result in some problems involving adequate representation of the varying interests found in very large districts, but would seem as capable of producing adequate representation as any other.

The second objection is handled in number 56 and deals with the question of whether or not the number of representatives will be too small to adequately represent all the interests to be found in the union. This objection is very probable regardless of the method of determining the number of representatives that will sit in the House of Representatives of the United Nations of Earth. Under either method suggested above the result will be a small number of representatives for a very large population, or a large number of interests being represented by a single representative. The question is whether or not, for example, two hundred and fifty million people, consisting of a wide range of diverse interests, could be adequately represented by one person. Considering the possibility of the creation of a permanent professional bureaucracy created to act as a research and consulting tool for designated representatives it seems that it would be possible. It is likely that representatives in a world government would find it imperative to establish large research and consulting organizations in their home districts to insure the flow of vital information back and forth. It may also be found necessary to elect only those candidates that have obtained specialized training, or experience, in the field of politics. The history of the US, Great Britain, China, and India seems to show that those who are responsible for representing very large populations with very diverse interests; and who have very little, or no, direct contact with their constituents, are still able to act effectively in their interest. This seems to be due to the fact that a vast majority of the interests found in any district, regardless of its size, are handled directly by the lesser subdivisions of government. Only those interests that affect a large segment of the district as a whole are pertinent to their representative in the general government. This would not change with the establishment of a world government. Each representative would still be concerned with only the larger issues that affected his constituency as a whole while the vast majority of the varying interests that affect his constituency would continue to be handled at the national or lower levels of government. It is at the lowest level of government, i.e., city, town, village, county, province, etc. that the peoples representatives are expected to have a detailed knowledge of all the varying interests. At each higher level of government the issues become more general and are supported by the knowledge of the lower levels of government, until at last only the issues of the widest interest are put before the general government. It is at the last level that the research and consulting staff become necessary to compile all the information available at the lower levels of government into a package of issues that affect the district or nation as a whole. For example, every person in any given member nation will have a common interest in obtaining the best roads, bridges, railroads, sanitary sewers, and water systems possible. The same would be true of the world's citizens, as a whole, in relation to the prevention and cleanup of environmental pollution, the conservation of natural resources, and the regulation of outer space, the open seas, and cyberspace. Every citizen, regardless of the nation in which they live, would have a common interest in the amount, and kind, of individual welfare that would be available, for example, what amount and type of relief would be available for those who become unemployed, disabled, or too old to work, etc. There does not appear to be any reason that a representative could not become quickly informed as to his constituency's interests in regard to these types of issues.

Number 57 presents the third objection, which claims that the members of the House of Representatives will all be drawn from the same class of society. The fear being expressed, according to the Federalist, is that if one class, regardless of which class, is able to garner all the power of government unto itself then the result will be an oligarchy. The arguments used against this objection do not extend beyond the safeguards that are to be found in the proposed constitution against such an event. This safeguard is essentially the fact that each representative is elected by the whole of their constituents and that the elections are held frequently. In the first case the representative elected is likely to represent a cross section of those who elect them; and second the frequency of election tends to bar the collusion of a large number of representatives. These arguments, however, do not answer the specific objection being offered, that is, that all representatives will tend to come from one class within the society. As we have seen the contention of some historians, such as Howard Zinn, is that the government from top to bottom was established with the conscious thought that all power would be controlled by a small number of wealthy individuals. It is true that throughout US history the vast majority of those that have served the public have come from the upper middle class and the upper classes. Indeed, a significant number of those who have served belonged to the professional caste of lawyers. It is certain that those most likely to be available for public service are those that are able to afford the time and money to run and serve. Today, for example, to run for election to even the lower levels of government in the US requires a considerable investment of time and money. Only those who are independently capable of giving the necessary time and money, or those who have gained the support of those who have the money, can expect to be successful candidates. At the higher levels of government the commitment in time and money is significantly larger and requires even more of each candidate. In most cases, at least in the US, it takes a commitment of time ranging into several years and a commitment of money running into the tens of millions of dollars. This puts these offices out of the reach of all but the very wealthy (probably the top one percent of the population); or limits the candidates to those that are chosen by the two political parties and those who support them financially. A quick survey of those who are currently serving in the House of Representatives, the Senate, and the elected offices of the executive branch, as well as, the members of the Supreme Court all tend to be independently wealthy individuals. In short, anyone who is interested in promoting a career in politics, especially in the areas that require election by the people, will tend to be a member of the upper class and capable of producing the leisure time to serve. It can, on the other hand, be argued that even though a large share of those elected to office have been from the upper class, this has not prevented the interests of all classes of society from being served. It can also be argued that class bias in office has led to a relatively slight amount of abuse within the government. The current system of nationalism may allow the problem represented by the third objection to take a more prominent role. For example, it may be that national leaders may be more capable of rallying their citizens in support of a particular issue to a greater extent than is possible for the governor of a state. This is not possible to determine in advance but there does not appear to be any reason to expect the world government to operate in this regard much differently than the US

One may not agree with the contentions made by Howard Zinn but it is necessary in this context to consider them. He contends that the US government from its inception has been ruled by an oligarchy of wealth. The argument extends not only to the fact that a large proportion of those serving at all levels of government are bound to the interests of this group, but that this group consciously conspired to rule exclusively in their own interests and drafted the constitution to make this rule possible. If Zinn is correct in his theory, then Hamilton and Madison are correct in their belief that mankind is not yet ready to assume self- government. Although examples, sometimes glaring examples, have been used to support the theory offered by Zinn, it is also true that when the people become aware of the wide scope being given a class they take action to eliminate the predominance of that class. The same can be said of the periodic ascendance of specific ideals, or movements, during US history, that is, when they have played out the role expected of them they are left to wither on the vine. In theory the groups presented to us by Zinn have consciously used their power to operate against the common good. The power of elect representatives in a democracy must be located somewhere and by definition in a democracy that is in the people. Faith must be held in the ability of the people, over the long term, to make accurate judgments concerning the character of those who they elect and a determination as to whether they truly represent their interests. The final, or ultimate, safeguard against the abuse of power, by any level of government, or any member of it, resides in the creation of a well-educated and responsible public. Regardless of the conspiracy claimed by Zinn the short history of the US, and the long history of Great Britain would seem to justify this faith in the public wisdom. As Zinn clearly points out, this does not mean that one class in the society, or one specific interest, will not at times predominate over all others, even sometimes contrary to the public good. What it does mean is that the best safeguard against a conspiratorial governing by one class or interest in opposition to all others is a representative democracy populated by well educated and responsible citizens.

Number 58 continues the arguments set forth above. Here it will suffice to set forth a short quote to give the flavor of the arguments used by the Federalist Papers to counter the objections that were raised along these lines.

> Experience will forever admonish them that, on the contrary, after securing a sufficient number for the purposes of safety, of local information, and of diffusive sympathy with the whole society, they will counteract their own views by every addition to their representatives. The countenance of the government may become more democratic, but the soul that animates it will be more oligarchic. The machine will be enlarged, but the fewer, and often the more secret, will be the springs by which its motions are directed.[1]

The point being, that the larger the body the more likely that it will be controlled by the secret maneuvers of a few individuals.

Numbers 59 and 60 present the question of whether or not the times, places, and manner of electing federal officials, with the exception of Senators, should reside with the federal government. It would be worth the effort for anyone who seriously objects to this power in the general government to read through the two numbers listed. The Federalist Papers simply asserts that this power must reside in the general government to insure its ability to provide for its own survival. It might now also be added that the method chosen, although changed, as we shall see, in regard to the president and the Senate, has led to no great ill effects or insoluble problems. Lately in the US there have been some questions raised about the validity of certain types of ballots, and about certain types of procedures. This, of course, must be considered when a decision is made as to the times, places, and manner of electing the officials of the general world government.

---

1 *The Federalist Papers*, No. 58, p. 181, Great Books of the Western World, Encyclopedia Britannica.

In number 61 Hamilton continues the arguments relating to the power of the federal government to control elections. Here he points out that the constitution only delegates the power to regulate the times, places, and manner of election; while the several states remain responsible for regulating the qualifications of those who hold themselves out for election, as well as the qualifications to obtain the right to vote. At that time the franchise was essentially restricted to white males who owned a specified amount of real property or its equivalent. Today the franchise is accorded to every citizen that has obtained the age of eighteen years. By constitutional amendment all of the various barriers erected by the states to limit the franchise have been removed with almost no exceptions. The same qualifications for the franchise that now exist in the US would be extended under the proposed constitution to all people living anywhere on Earth including those convicted of treason. The only exception would be those who are truly mentally incompetent to exercise the right to vote. Even in these cases a system of proxy voting might be devised to protect their interests. The general government would have the same power of regulating the times, places, and manner of election regarding all offices that require election. It is unlikely that any objections will be raised against the establishment of a uniform time, a uniform ballot, and a uniform manner for conducting the elections. This does not mean that disagreements will not arise over any specific time, place, or manner of conducting elections that might be chosen. The goal, of course, is to come up with a time, place, and manner of conducting the election that allows the greatest number of people possible to exercise the franchise in the most convenient manner possible. This would include safety from any form of coercion in casting of individual votes. This discussion ends the coverage by the Federalist Papers relating to the creation of a House of Representatives.

Number 62 begins the discussion of the provisions relating to the creation of the Senate. This discussion centers on five issues. First, the qualifications for senators; second, the appointment of senators by the state legislatures; three, the equal number of senators to be allowed each state; four, the number and length of service granted to the senate; and five, the powers to be vested in the senate. In regard to the qualifications of a senator the limitations are again very simple. A senator must have reached the age of thirty years, a senator must have been a citizen of the US for nine years; and a senator must reside in the state that appoints him at the time of his appointment. In the case of the proposed world government the qualifications will be the same with the exception of the nine year residency provision. The appointment of senators by the legislative bodies of the several states, or nations in our case, would be altered only to read that they would be appointed by the several nations under whatever procedure was chosen by that nation rather than by the legislative body. This would take into account those nations that do not currently have independent legislative bodies. The intention of this provision of the constitution was to allow a method whereby each individual state would have equal representation in the Senate. This was an obvious compromise between the large states and the small states based on the grievance of the small states in regard to representation in the House of Representatives. The same intention is being developed in regard to the Senate of the world government, that is, that each nation will be recognized in its corporate capacity and be granted equal representation in the Senate. The US after a period of time had passed determined that it was best to allow the election of senators directly by the people by means of secret ballot. As a result the states lost their power to determine the qualifications of those who would serve in the Senate, and it may also have resulted in the election of less well qualified candidates. In our case the same shift is not recommended for two reasons, one, that the quality of those serving as senators will most likely be consistently higher than if elected by ballot, and two, the nations must be acknowledged in their corporate capacity in some part of the government to remain independently sovereign in relation to the general government, e.g., to maintain a republican form of government. The appointment of senators by the several nations seems to be the only manner in which the desired diversity in national identity, cultural distinctiveness, and religious diversity could be maintained peacefully. If, in fact, writers such as Francis Fukuyama are accurate in their assessment of the importance of national identity and cultural diversity, not only for the citizens of the several nations, but for the nations themselves, then it is imperative that the nations be recognized in their corporate capacity. The method of appointing senators was an easy matter in the early US as all the states had a representative legislative body. The same is not true in regard to the existing nations, some of which have dependent legislative bodies or no real legislative bodies at all. For this reason a more flexible system for appointments must be established. For example, in some nations the appointment to the Senate would be made by a dictator or by a monarch or other executive leader; while in yet others the appointment would be made by a judicial body or a religious tribunal. In any case the appointment must be allowed to be made by whatever method has been accepted by the people to cover such events. In regard to the proposed equality in senators that would be allowed each nation, most of the relevant points have already been established above. In our case only one major chance would be put into effect. In the US Constitution each state was allowed two senators but only one vote on each issue. In our case each nation would also have two senators but each senator would be authorized to vote their conscience on each issue. This would allow any individual senator the right to vote against the interest of his nation should they feel that their nation was acting in opposition to the public good. In regard to the term of service the US Constitution allowed a six-year term with one third of the senate beginning up for reappointment every two years. This would be the same in our case with the first Senate being divided into three classes. The first class would serve two years, the second four years, and the third six years. The division would be carried out by the Senate itself once assembled. It was conceded that the method of appointment, rather than election, would make it the interest of the state to appoint the most qualified individuals it could find. Normally this would amount to appointing people who had already shown their virtue to the people, either through their legislative experience within the state, or some other public distinction. The system of appointment seems to tend to result in the best of the best being appointed. It is logical that the best qualified persons should be trusted with longer terms of service to allow them to display their talents. It was intended that the Senate would provide a measure of stability in the general government in regard to legislation. The six year term allows three times more time for a senator to acquire the needed knowledge to judge the worth of any piece of legislation that might be proposed. In our case the total number of senators would be about four hundred with one hundred and thirty three being up for reappointment every two years. It is this writers opinion that senators would be no more likely, and maybe less likely, to serve multiple terms under a system of appointment than under a system of public election. In the US a relatively large number of senators have served multiple terms, some even serving six or seven consecutive terms, or thirty five years. The discussion of the powers to be granted the Senate was postponed to number 64.

John Jay is believed to have written number 64 and begins the discussion of the powers that are to be given to the Senate. This number looks at the concurrent powers of the Senate and the executive branch. These powers are two in number, the power to declare war and peace and to make treaties. The power to make treaties, assuming a unanimous membership in the world union would no longer be needed. In all cases where treaties were used under the system of nationalism the issues involved would be matters of a contractual nature, or a matter of general regulations issued by the general government. These same issues would as a matter of course fall under the judicial power of the general government whenever a dispute arose that involved them. If the situation at the time of the inception of the world union was one where one or more nations remained outside the union then the general government would need the power to make treaties. As with the system in the US the constitution could make this power subject to the approval of the Senate.

Numbers 65 and 66 treat the remaining powers that were to be delegated to the Senate. These powers included the giving of advice and consent on the appointment of all federal officials subject to appointment, including the Supreme Court justices; the power of advice and consent to the declaring of war and peace by the executive branch. Also included was the power to try all cases of impeachment brought by the House of Representatives. Under the Constitution of the US, as well as the one proposed here, the power to try cases of impeachment is vested in the Senate as a check and balance of the power to impeach which had been delegated to the House of Representatives. It was the result of following the old adage that a man cannot be trusted to be the judge in his own case. A further check on the power of impeachment, as well as to check the power of trying impeachment cases, was added when the president was the one being impeached. In this case the Chief Justice of the Supreme Court would be required to preside over the proceedings. The Senate, therefore, would be allowed to try all cases of impeachment, even against one of its own members, which would, of course, allow them to sit in judgment in their own cause of action. The only other point to be made is that throughout US history the charge of impeachment has rarely been brought. It has, however, been brought, or threatened, more often recently than in the past. In most cases when impeachment is brought, or seriously threatened, the person involved resigns the office rather than face a trial in the Senate; as was the case with Richard Nixon the then sitting president of the United States. This would likely be the case in regard to the same power in the world union as impeachment bars the holding of any other office, while resignation does not.

In relation to the power of advice and consent it is applicable to two different types of actions, first, the executive power to declare war and peace, coupled with the power to make treaties, and the executive power to appoint all federal officers subject to appointment. Under the US Constitution, as well as the one proposed here, the president (executive branch) is given the sole power to appoint all federal officers. A check and balance to this power was granted to the Senate by giving the power of advice and consent. The power to appoint includes all major executive branch offices, such as department heads, cabinet ministers, etc., as well as the judges and justices of the federal judicial system. The power of advice and consent given to the Senate was intended to be a check and balance on the executive power of appointment. The Senate cannot force the executive branch, especially the president, to appoint any particular person to any particular office. However, they can force the president, or other executive officer, to keep appointing people to the office until one is selected that will meet with the approval of the Senate. Once again this system has operated throughout US history in a relatively efficient manner. There have been times when appointments have met with very stiff opposition, in some cases resulting in the candidate with-drawing their name from consideration, and in others with them being taken out of consideration by the vote of the Senate. This process is also closely tied to the development of a two party system in the United States. The president will as a matter of policy normally appoint people from within his own party for office. If a majority of the membership of the Senate is also in the control of the same party appointments tend to go rather smoothly. If the Senate majority is controlled by the opposite party then appointments tend to be a more delicate process. In the case of federal judges, and the justices of the Supreme Court, the opposition or approval of appointments tends to be based on the relative strength of conserva-tive and liberal philosophical political ideologies. Because of the term of good behavior granted judges and justices the federal court system has often been out of step with the general level of conservatism or liberalism in the society as a whole. This has over the period of US history acted as an unintended check and balance on the occasional control of the other two branches by one or the other political ideology.

In conclusion it should be noted that the Senate's powers, in important in-stances, are concurrent with that of the other two branches in connection with the intention of making the Senate a basis of stability within the government. Most of the intended checks and balances are situated within the Senate. This is usually given as one of the main reasons that the power to appoint Senators should remain with the several nations in their corporate capacity rather being subject to a popular vote directly by the people as is now the case in the US

Number 67 of the Federalist Papers at first sight seems to be a little out of order in relation to the progression followed in the other articles. Instead of moving directly to a discussion of the powers granted to the executive branch as expected the discussion centers on only one isolated power of the executive branch. This power is that of filling vacancies in the executive branch while the Senate is in recess. This power does not need much discussion as the vacancies, at times, will need to be filled even though the Senate is in recess. The president is given the power to fill the vacancies which occur during such a period, but only for the duration of the recess. Upon the next session of the Senate that appointment will be handled in the same manner as if it had occurred while the Senate is in session. In our case the scheduled recess of congress will be so short that it will not matter in a vast majority of the vacancies whether they are filled before the next session or not.

In number 68 Hamilton begins the discussion of the powers that will be granted to the executive branch. Due to the lack of discussion, or lack of objections raised, to this issue in 1790, in this case alone the number will be quoted in its entirety, and then analyzed in relation to the circumstances that face the proposed constitution that has been presented for a world government.

"The mode of appointment of the chief magistrate of the United States is almost the only part of the system, of any consequence, which has escaped censure, or which has received the slightest mark of approbation from its opponents. The most plausible of these, who has appeared in print, has even deigned to admit that the election of the president is pretty well guarded. I venture somewhat further, and hesitate not to affirm, that if the manner of it be not perfect, it is at least excellent. It unites in an eminent degree all the advantages, in union of which was to be wished for."

"It was equally desirable that the immediate election should be made by men more capable of analyzing the qualities adapted to the station, and acting under circumstances favorable to deliberation, and to a judicious combination of all the reasons and inducements which were proper to govern the choice. A small number of persons, selected by their fellow citizens from the general mass, will be most likely to possess the information and discernment requisite to such complicated investigations."

"It was also peculiarly desirable to afford as little opportunity as possible to tumult and disorder. This evil was not least to be directed in the election of a magistrate who was to have so important an agency in the administration of the government as the president of the United States. But the precautions which have been so happily concerted in the system under consideration, promise an effectual security against mischief. The choice of *several*, to form an intermediate body of electors, will be much less apt to convulse the community with any extraordinary or violent movements than the choice of *one* who was himself to be the final object of the public wishes. And as the electors chosen in each state are to assemble and vote in the state in which they are chosen, this detached and divided situation will expose them much less to heats and ferments, which might be communicated from them to the people, than if they were all to be convened at one time in one place."

"Nothing was more to be desired than that every practicable obstacle should be opposed to cabal, intrigue, and corruption. These most deadly adversaries of republican government might naturally have been expected to make their approaches from more than one quarter, but chiefly from the desire of foreign powers to gain an improper ascendant in our councils. How could they better gratify this than be raising a creature of their own to the chief magistracy of the union? But the convention guarded against all danger of this sort with the most provident and judicious attention. They have not made the appointment of the president to depend on any pre-existing bodies of men, who might be tampered with beforehand to prostitute their votes; but they have referred it in the first instance to an immediate act of the people of America, to be exerted in the choice of persons for the temporary and sole purpose of making the appointment. And they have excluded from eligibility to this trust all those who from situation might be suspected of too great devotion to the president in office. No senator, representative, or other person holding a position of trust or profit under the United States can be of the numbers of the electors. This without corrupting the body of the people, the immediate agents in the election will at least enter upon the task free from any sinister bias. Their transient existence, and their detached situation, already taken notice of, afford satisfactory prospect of their continuing so to the conclusion of it. The business of corruption, when it is to embrace so considerable a number of men, requires time as well as means. Nor would it be found easy suddenly to embark them, dispersed as they would be over the thirteen states, in any combinations founded upon motives which, though they could properly be denominated corrupt, might yet be of a nature to mislead them from their duty."

"Another and no less important desideratum was that the executive should be independent for his continuance in office on all but the people themselves. He might otherwise be tempted to sacrifice his duty to his complaisance for those whose favor was necessary to the duration of his official consequence. This advantage will also be secured by making his reelection to depend on a special body of representatives, deputed by the society for the single purpose of making the important choice."

"All these advantages will happily combine in the plan devised by the convention; which is, that the people of each state shall choose a number of persons as electors, equal to the number of senators and representatives of each in the national government, and the person who may happen to have a majority of the whole number of votes will be the president. But as a majority of the votes might not always happen to center in one man, and as it might be unsafe to permit less than a majority to be conclusive, it is provided that, in such a contingency, the House of Representatives shall select out of the candidates who shall have the five highest number of votes, the man who in their opinion may be best qualified for the office."

"The process of election affords a moral certainty that the office of president will never fall to the lot; or any man who is not in an eminent degree endowed with the requisite qualifications. Talents for low intrigue and the little arts of popularity may alone suffice to elevate a man to the first honours in a single state; but it will require other talents, and a different kind of merit, to establish him in the esteem and confidence of the whole union, or of so considerable a portion of it as would be necessary to make him a successful candidate for the distinguished office of President of the United States. It will not be too strong to say that there will be a constant probability of seeing the station filled by characters pre-eminent for ability and virtue. And this will be thought no inconsiderable recommendation of the constitution by those who are able to estimate the share which the executive in every government must necessarily have in its good or ill administration. Though we cannot acquiesce in the political heresy of the poet who says—

For forms of government let fools contest —
That which is best administered is best.

Yet we may safely pronounce that the true test of a good government is it aptitude and tendency to produce a good administration.

The Vice-President is to be chosen in the same manner with the President; with this difference, that the Senate is to do, in respect with the former, what is to be done by the House of Representatives, in respect to the latter.

The appointment of an extraordinary person, as vice-president, has been objected to as superfluous, if not mischievous. It has been alleged, that it would have been preferable to have authorized the Senate to elect out of their own body an officer answering the description. But two considerations seem to justify the ideas of the convention in this respect. One is, that to secure at all times the possibility of a definite resolution of the body, it is necessary that the president should have only a casting vote. And to take the senator of any state from his seat as a senator, to place him in that of the president of the senate, would be to exchange, in regard to the state from which he came, a constant for a contingent vote. The other consideration is that as the vice-president he may occasionally become a substitute for the President, in the supreme executive magistracy. All the reasons which recommend the mode of election proscribed for the one apply with great if not equal force to the manner of appointing the other. It is remarkable that in this, as in most other instances, the objection which is made would lie against the constitution of this state. We have not a lieutenant governor, chosen by the people at large, who presides in the Senate, and is the constitutional substitute for the governor in causalities similar to those which would authorize the vice-president to exercise the authorities and discharge the duties of the President. (Publius)[1]

It must be stated initially that the United States did not adhere to the constitutionally proscribed method of electing the president. By 1820 the system had become something far different than that argued by Hamilton. The United States still technically elects the president through the votes of the electors of the several states. Those who serve as electors in each state still serve in a number equal to the total number of senators and representatives from that state. The method of electing the people who will serve as electors, however, has changed considerably. In some states this is done by convention, that is, the party who wins the state primary election is assured of receiving that state's electoral vote at the conclusion of the process. In other cases, the party selects those who will serve as electors without the intervention of a public vote. At any rate, the electors

---

1 *The Federalist Papers*, No. 68, pp. 205-207, Great Books of the Western World, Encyclopedia Britannica.

of each party then meet in convention and select the persons that they want to run for the offices of president and vice-president. The choices of the two parties, and the candidates of independent third parties, if any, and if capable of qualifying, then run for the offices on the basis of a general public election. The person who receives the most votes in each state, regardless of his party, takes all the electoral votes of that state. The person running for vice-president does not run independently but as a member of the party ticket, or as the running mate of the president. In any case, the electors are no longer free to vote for whomever they feel is the most qualified person, but must vote in a block for whoever wins the majority of votes in their state. Therefore, for all essential purposes, the two political parties, that is, the Republicans and Democrats, select the electors who will serve, the person who will run for president and vice-president, and can effectively block any third party, or independent, candidates from gaining the offices. This has led to some strange results in recent elections. For example, in his first term George W. Bush lost the election in terms of the popular vote, but won the election in terms of gathering the majority of electoral votes. In essence, one party can win all the electoral votes of a state, even though they may not have garnered a majority of the public vote in that state, and can win the election without winning the majority of the popular vote. The actual electoral vote is a matter of course; whichever party has won enough of the popular vote to garner the majority of electoral votes wins the election. The fact that the popular vote does not necessarily determine the election, coupled with the fact that a few key states are capable of producing enough electoral votes to constitute a majority, has led to strong calls to abandon the electoral system in favor of a straight popular vote, or at least, to reform the electoral system so that the people again control who serves as electors. The current US practice is a clumsy mixture of the electoral system and the system of popular vote. Few find this mixture palatable. Either a true electoral system, such as that proscribed by the constitution, should be used or the constitution should be amended to allow for the use of straight popular vote. The initial change was occasioned by the suspicion that was raised as to influence peddling in the House of Representatives over the election of Thomas Jefferson the third president of the United States.

The dominance of the two political parties, i.e., the Republicans and the Democrats, both in the selection of candidates for office, and the electors who will elect them, has removed the people at large from any significant voice in who will represent them in both the executive and legislative branches of government. The current system seems to relieve the candidates from the need for any outstanding qualifications, except for that of status within the party, and allows the elections for congress and the Presidency to become mere popularity contests. What is ironic is that the use of popular elections for the Senate and for the executive magistracy has forced the candidates to expend very large amounts of time and money to gain the nomination of their party and to garner the vote of the public. This has left them open to the influence of money interests such as corporate sponsors and special interest groups.

Probably the most telling example is that of George W. Bush and Albert Gore. George W. Bush lost the popular election to Gore but the electoral vote came down to the votes of the electoral contingent from Florida. The popular election count in Florida came under suspicion because of some suspected faulty voting machines. At the time the brother of George W. Bush was the governor of Florida, and had, of course, appointed the director of the voting commission for Florida who had to certify the popular vote count, and thereby, the electoral vote. In this case the vote was certified to have gone to George W. Bush, although all of the contested votes had not yet been counted. Gore eventually conceded the election to Bush rather than to take the issue before the Supreme Court. This decision by Gore, or his party, merely delayed the final decision on the fate of the electoral system. The problems will reappear, probably in even more distressing ways, and at some date will need to be resolved. In the constitution proposed here for the establishment of a world government the option to return to a pure electoral system has been taken for the reasons set forth by Hamilton, and in response to the US system currently in place. It is felt that this is the only practicable manner, in which the evils of US history can be countered, however, the convention, with much wiser and informed minds, may find a solution that has not occurred to this author. It is also significant to take note of the manner in which representatives are qualified to sit in the European Union and its various offices. In this case the personnel are appointed by the member nations themselves with only the European Parliament standing for public election. In many ways this is comparable to the system proposed in the constitution proposed for a world government.

This issue is of paramount importance in relation to the project of creating a world union. At the very least, it appears from current world conditions, that at least initially, the persons selected as candidates for president and vice-president will not be selected by two dominant political parties. They will be selected, by whatever method is chosen, from a world that contains a wide variety of interests, and that will more closely represent the national interests from where they come than the electors of the United States. It can be expected that the electoral system will be in our case what it was originally intended to be under the early US Constitution. The people of each nation will select a number of people solely for the purpose of nominating the persons they would like to see occupy the two top executive offices of the union. The people chosen by the several nations to accomplish this task may be chosen by whatever system is in force in the several nations to accomplish such tasks. In some cases, this will be by nomination by the top executive officer, that is, a monarch or despot. In others, it will be selection by a religious tribunal such as would be expected in Muslim dominated governments; in still others, by election of the people in nations which currently operate under democratic governments. The point being that each nation would have the right to nominate for president and vice-president of the world union the persons that they thought the most fit to hold the office. From this election the persons who obtained the majority of votes would become president and vice-president. Should no one receive a majority of votes the president would be chosen by the House of Representatives from the five persons who received the most votes; and the vice-president would be chosen in the Senate using the same procedure as in the House of Representatives. In our case the constitution would provide that each nation nominate two persons for each office, one of which must be a person not resident in the nation nominating. A uniform time, place, and manner would be proscribed for the casting of these votes, which would be done in the nation in which the electors reside. The votes would then be sent to the speaker of the House of Representatives who would count the votes before a full joint session of congress. This system has two major benefits, among a host of others; first, it will eliminate the huge cost of election campaigns as they are now conducted in the United States. This will include a reduction of the influence of special interest groups and corporate interests who expect favors for their contributions of money and votes. Second, it will isolate the two offices from undue influence from organized political parties and organized national efforts to effect policy. It should also contribute to the stemming of the remarkable drop in voter participation in elections recently noted in the US, supposedly the most democratic of all nations.

The question now arises as to the method that the electors will use to choose those they wish to nominate for the two top executive offices. Do they choose anyone they deem to be fit, one from their own nation, and one from another nation? Do they select from a list of candidates provided by some independent body selected for the sole purpose of creating a list of qualified candidates? In either case how will the candidates be nominated? The current experience of the US in using the popular vote for the selection of candidates does not appear to be a particularly effective one. In the early stages of US history, however, the legislatures of the several states were responsible for the selection of candidates that would be selected from by the electors. In our case the several nations, under whatever system existed for such purposes, might select the candidates from which the electors might choose. The electors would then choose the two who they felt the most qualified and who they felt should be certified for election. Each nation would then certify its candidates and send them to the speaker of the House of Representatives by a specified date. The speaker would then count the votes before a full session of congress, etc.

It seems likely that whatever system is chosen by the individual nations for selection of the candidates for the two top executive offices that a committee nominated for the sole purpose of producing a list of qualified candidates would be used. This is an accepted procedure used by US corporations for obtaining qualified candidates for the position of CEO, and by US universities to produce a list of qualified candidates for the top executive position in their institutions. It could be recommended that a relatively short time period be assigned to the committee in its task of producing a list of qualified candidates. This method would most likely result in the selection of the most qualified candidates in relation to the particular interests of the nation involved. It would also most likely result in the presentation of candidates that fit the needs of a large number of nations who had the same or very similar interests. It would eliminate the need for expensive and time consuming popular elections, while at the same time preserving the underlying principles of liberal democracy. The electors, of course, under this system would be unrestricted in their vote for those on the list of candidates that they thought the most qualified. It would be most efficient and cost effective to have the electoral vote conducted in each nation on a uniform date and time, and in a manner that would require certification and delivery to the speaker of the House of Representatives on a date certain.

If the electoral system, or some altered version of it, is not chosen the only other method of determining the wishes of the public is a general ballot. This is what is being considered in the US to replace the current mixture of popular vote and electoral system in place. The use of a direct vote system in the environment of a world union would seem to pose very difficult logistical problems. Unlike the US where there are two highly organized and well financed political parties legally entitled to select the candidates and issues that will be heard exists; in our situation the existence of many different political parties, with no legal power to select candidates or issues exists. In such a scenario the use of a direct public election of the two top executive offices would seem to lead to utter chaos. This chaos would be most clearly represented by the tremendous amount of time and money a candidate would need to commit to get their "message" before the public.

If the current US experience can be used as a guide, the time involved could run into a number of years that would exceed the length of term in office, and the cost would run into the billions of dollars. It is therefore suggested that a committee be nominated every four years for the sole purpose of producing a list of candidates that are qualified for the office from the applications that they receive for the position. Once the committee has selected from the applications submitted the most qualified candidates for the two positions; the full congress would then select the five most qualified candidates, in their opinion, for each office and these five candidates would then appear on a general ballot. The public would then vote on the person, from this list of five, that they felt most qualified for each office. This vote would be certified and sent to the speaker. If one candidate received a majority vote for each office then the election would be complete. If not, then the full congress would certify the two highest votes and those persons would be returned to the general ballot for a reelection based upon the most votes regardless of majority status. In any way that one attempts to look at this question the most clumsy and inappropriate method seems to be a direct popular vote. It is certainly possible to protect the people's position as the sole, or final repository of power without involving them in a direct exercise of that power. That is, in fact, the whole meaning, or purpose of representative democracy, and the main principal underlying the ideology of liberal democracy. Whatever system is chosen to determine the candidates for the two top executive offices it cannot be stressed enough that the decision is crucial to the success of the proposed world union.

In number 69, Hamilton begins the discussion of the powers to be vested in the office of president. The power is to be vested in a single magistrate, whose term of office will be four years, with eligibility to hold office as long as the confidence of the people is maintained, that is, there is no restriction on reappointment to the office except the vote of the people for electors. The president, and all other executive officers, would be subject to impeachment proceedings as pointed out earlier. They would also be subject to indictment and conviction for any crimes committed while in office. Such trials and convictions would be prosecuted in the ordinary course of the law after impeachment or resignation from office.

The president would have the power to veto any legislation that he saw fit prior to their becoming law. Under the proposed constitution this power must be exercised within ten days, excluding holidays and Sundays, and must be accompanied by his objections when returned to the house of congress which initiated the bill. The veto, however, can be overruled by reconsideration by congress and passing the bill with a two-thirds vote of each house. If the bill is signed by the president, or his veto is overcome, or the bill is not returned within the specified ten days the bill becomes law.

The president would also have the power of Commander in Chief of all the military forces assigned to the Union. He would under this power have the direction, through those of his own choice, of the use of the military forces in case of war or internal insurrection. The president would under this power have the right to put into service with the Union any forces that exist in the form of national militias, if any. The president could also commit these forces for a period of sixty days without the advice and consent of congress, but for no longer period. The congress is allowed the check and balance of advice and consent, and a limitation on the length that financing is allowed, that is, appropriations can last no longer than two years without being renewed.

The president would have the power to grant pardons and reprieves for all offenses committed against the union, except for impeachment.

The president would have the power to submit recommendations to congress at any time for laws that the president deems necessary. In this connection the president would have the duty once a year to meet with congress and present to them the state of the union.

As we saw earlier the president would have the power to appoint all executive officers, make treaties, appoint ambassadors, consuls, and adjuncts, and to receive the same from nations outside the union, and to declare war and peace, with the advice and consent of congress.

The president would have the power to convene one or both houses of congress during any period of recess should the president see fit.

Lastly, the president would have the duty to faithfully execute all the laws of the general government and to create the necessary departments to fulfill that duty.

These powers were not brought under attack by those who opposed the constitution and were, therefore, merely listed in the Federalist Papers. In our case it is only necessary to point out that the powers reflecting treaties, contracts, ambassadors, consuls, etc. would only come into play if there were one or more nations that did not join the union. It is likely that if a significant number of nations remain outside the union after ratification that the project would not be instituted. The remaining powers have all become a stable part of all executive branches found in existing representative democracies, and in some cases include additional powers. These additional powers may be incorporated into the proposed constitution should the convention deem it necessary.

In numbers 70 and 71 Hamilton explains the ingredients that make for an active and effective executive. They are according to Hamilton as follow: unity, duration, adequate support, and competent powers. Unity, in Hamilton's point of view, means the settling of all powers given to the executive branch solely in the president. Duration is accomplished by being able to extend the initial four year term indefinitely with a maintaining of the confidence of the people. The current system in the US has left this factor and replaced with a mandatory leaving of office after two terms of office or eight years service. Any division of the powers of the president deprives the public of its two main sources of safety, i.e., the restrictions placed on executive action by public opinion, which cannot be applied unless the pressure can be effectively directed, and second, the opportunity of discovering mismanagement of the executive office, i.e., someone must be responsible for the mismanagement whether personally responsible or not. Any constitutional limitation on the service of any individual as president also limits the benefits that can be derived from experience and superior talents. Under the current system in the US the powers have remained undivided, but the duration of the office has been restricted to eight years. This restriction has shown that it not only deprives the executive branch of superior talent and experience, as expressed by Hamilton, but also severely limits the president's ability to fulfill the duties of the office during his last term. In addition, recent presidents have shown a clear lack of the endurance needed to accomplish an active and effective administration over a period of eight years, largely due to a lack of support during the final four years. Recent presidents have also shown a remarkable pandering to the interests responsible for their election. Some have also shown something less than a tolerable moral fiber while in office. The last few US presidents have maintained a public opinion rating favorable to their service record of less than fifty percent during most of their terms in office. While it is debatable that the restriction on the duration of the term served has been the main cause of these issues it has more than likely contributed a significant share. Four years is a very short time to allow for the growth of expertise in the president, especially in the areas of handling the professional media, negotiating desired legislation through congress and passage into law, and the handling of long term social problems. The result has been a massive dependence of the president on the professional bureaucracy, which remains in office regardless of who is president, and is unaffected by public pressure. The projects that have taken up the time of the presidents serving over the last few decades have been so vast that they could not even be properly studied in one eight year term. These projects, therefore, are dependent for planning, implementation, and completion on two main factors, one, the duration of the professional bureaucracy, and the continuation in office of the same political party over the terms of several presidents. The latter, however, cannot be guaranteed either in the fact or in the execution of similar political philosophy. In 1789 the Federalist feared that the legislative powers were most likely to upset the balance obtained in the constitution. Today, however, through the use of a professional bureaucracy, and two dominant political parties, it is probably the executive branch that is most likely to upset the balance. Although the bureaucracy is the adequate support asked for by Hamilton, it appears that it has grown so large and complicated that no president, in the time allowed, will be able to gather the experience, or have the talent, to produce an effective administration.

In the case presented here regarding the calling of a convention for the establishment of world government the convention will have an opportunity to rethink the powers that might be granted the three branches of government. It may be that more powers and duties will need to be delegated to one or another of the three branches. It may also be possible that additional powers may need to be set aside for the national governments to give them the flexibility of enforcing the rules, regulations, and laws passed by the general government. If the national governments were given the primary duty of implementing and enforcing the various laws, edicts, and regulations passed by the general government, using the bureaucracies already in place to implement and enforce their own laws, one very large portion of the need for a general bureaucracy would be removed. In the US currently the states, as well as, the federal government, have large bureaucracies that essentially duplicate the same responsibilities, for example, tax collection. It might be possible to greatly reduce this important waste of assets. In the end, the failure, if it is a failure, of modern representative democracy on the national level can be traced directly to its assumption of duties and responsibilities that are best left to local governmental agencies. It can only be hoped that the creation of a world government will not add another layer to this inefficient way of conducting government business.

In number 72 Hamilton presents the Federalist arguments for allowing the people, in their constitutional right of voting, to continue in office as president anyone who they feel has earned and merited that continuation without limit. The most telling argument presented by Hamilton revolves around the mutability of measures and conduct that always seems to accompany a rapid change in positions of trust. The current situation in the US is a good example of the thrust of the arguments presented. The president is limited to two terms whether the terms are served consecutively or not. It appears that this limitation arose from two major sources. First the fact that George Washington voluntarily limited himself to two terms, which stood as a precedent for all following presidents until Franklin Roosevelt. Roosevelt was elected to four consecutive terms and actually served as president for twelve years before his death. The justification given in Roosevelt's case was the fact that he served during the Great Depression and during World War II, and that it would have been dangerous to change leadership during such extreme challenges. The rancor that was generated by Roosevelt's four terms was played out quickly in party politics. In 1951, only seven years after Roosevelt's death, and only three years after the end of the last term for which he was elected, a constitutional amendment was passed limiting the term to a maximum of eight years. Recent administrations however that have served since 1951 clearly show that the effective service of the president has been reduced to four years or the first term. In the second term the president can quickly become what is affectionately called a "lame duck" administration. There has also been evidence of a high degree of mutability in the policies of succeeding administrations just as Hamilton had feared. Eight years as mentioned earlier, is not enough time to expect consistent handling of problems that tend to stretch over decades such as foreign relations, economic recessions, depressions and booms, and social problems such as women's rights and discrimination. By removing the choice of who will be president out of the hands of the people it can be expected that the selection will be made by well organized well financed political parties and interest groups. It, of course, also results in the unnecessary loss of experience and talent that might otherwise be put to good use.

In 73, Hamilton presents some conclusions concerning the compensation to be paid the president. He asserts that such compensation should be, at least, adequate to support the person holding office for the time served, and that this compensation should put him above the necessity of any other independent income. Currently the compensation of the president of the US is $400,000 a year for the rest of his or her life. In relation to the salaries of top corporate officers, sports figures, and entertainers this is minimal to say the least. It is not even certain that this amount is capable of independently sustaining the president while he is in office. Most presidents were wealthy prior to taking office or this might have been brought forward as a problem. It would be hoped that the world constitutional convention would take a close look at the compensation question, although it seems unlikely that the compensation should be specified in the constitution itself. Whatever the compensation determined amounts too it is likely that no one will object if it appears to be reasonable in relation to other positions of comparable service such as university and corporate officers.

Hamilton looks next at the condition extended that the president be armed with competent powers. He looks first at the president's power of veto. He begins by recognizing that such a veto must be either absolute or qualified. He accepts the arguments of history especially that of the Polish diet that an absolute veto gives more power to the executive than is proper to safeguard the public interest. He accepts the dictum that a qualified veto, as expressed in the constitution, allows for the reconsideration of questionable legislation, and requires a rethinking of its fulfillment of the public good. The qualified veto has been very successful in fulfilling its intended duty in all cases where it has been used in particular in the US

In numbers 74 through 77 Hamilton treats of the other powers granted to the executive by the constitution. Hamilton argues first that putting the power of commander in chief in the hands of one person is necessary to insure consistency in planning and tactics. The same is true of the power of reprieve and pardon. It is unlikely that any question will arise that the above powers be settled in the executive branch, as it is the established practice in every form of national government. The question will arise most likely from extensions of this power to cope with modern events. Historically the military power of a nation or union was to be used only in case of invasion by a foreign nation, or in case of internal insurrection. It has, however, been suggested here that the same power be used to deal with several other problem areas. In our case this would include random acts of violence (such as those today associated with political acts like that of 9-11-2001), illegal drug cartel activities, illegal abuse of the cyber space, catastrophic natural disasters, and many others. In these cases it appears that the most effective method of dealing with these problems is to settle all power to plan and react in one executive leader. The questions will probably arise over the extent of the power available to the executive in such cases and whether or not the powers granted would infringe on the right of individual privacy. These are not easy questions by any means and some may not be capable of an answer up front but only from experience. In 75 Hamilton treats the executive power to make treaties, which has been covered in detail above. In 76 the power of appointment is discussed, which again has been covered earlier. The only note that should be added here is that the system outlined in the US Constitution has worked successfully at least until recently. The last two decades, however, have shown that attempts to unduly reward party members with positions have brought serious problems. There appears in the US to be more concern with forwarding a specific political ideological agenda than with actual qualifications for the position. This, of course, makes appointments difficult to get approval for in the Senate if a different political ideological position is in the majority there. For example, the early nominations made by George W. Bush all seemed to be motivated by the desire to insure a conservative legal bias in the court. The candidates may also have been qualified for the position, but their political philosophy made it difficult for the president to get approval from a Senate that held a different political position. As a result the attempt to put extreme right wing conservatives on the court was defeated and Bush was forced to nominate more moderate conservatives to get approval.

It is likely that the president of the world government, who will have the same power of appointment, will also attempt to nominate those that most closely approximate his own political philosophy. In this case, at least initially, this will probably not be connected with any specific party affiliation, but rather, only known personal ideological beliefs. It is probable that in some cases that the world Senate will also oppose the nominations on the basis of personal political convictions. It is difficult to see how these two circumstances can be avoided. Without the restriction of party affiliations, however, it is likely that such differences would be focused on the qualifications for the position rather than personal political philosophy. Occasional disagreements between the president and the Senate concerning the fitness of any specific individual to hold the position for which they are nominated cannot be avoided. This is too be applauded as the power includes judges, Supreme Court justices, the heads of all executive departments, and the major advisory positions to the president. As such it is a very important power and requires that the most attention possible be devoted to obtaining those best qualified to serve. On the other hand, it is equally important that Senate confirmation also be based on the merits of the candidate for the position and little, if anything, else. If the selection committee method is used to produce a list of candidates, and we are correct in assuming that a two party system will not evolve, the nominations, and confirmation hearings, will under normal circumstances be made on the basis of merit alone.

The remaining powers of the executive branch did not occasion any objections either in 1789 nor does it seem likely that they will in 2009. Little is said about them in the Federalist Papers and nothing more will be added here, with the exception of one power, that is, the duty to faithfully execute the laws of the union. This duty has in large part been responsible for the exponential growth of the federal and state bureaucracies. This duty has also been responsible for the tendency in republican democracies for the reserved powers in the lower governments becoming concentrated in the general government. For example, the enforcement of the laws, regulations, and edits involving interstate trade, the general welfare, the tax laws, and many others of the same nature have resulted in the growth of both federal and state bureaucracies whose sole purpose is to administer enforcement of these laws. In the US, and most likely in most nations, this tendency has been accelerated by the general governments attempt to not only supervise the enforcement but to involve itself in the actual day-to-day enforcement activities. This attempt has alone been responsible for the creation of numerous agencies, departments, and their bureaucracies to accomplish the desired goal of enforcement. It is an accepted dictum in the US that if you wish to have a project to be handled in the worse way, in relation to cost and efficiency, give the project to the federal government. For example, the federal response to the devastation of Hurricane Katrina was a classic example of the dictum. The personnel used were those with the least knowledge of the needs involved, they were the most distant from the actual sight of the damage, and they were the least concerned about the planning, implementation, and delivery of the relief provided. As a result there was a vast waste of effort, assets, and good will. The worst affect was that the aid was never delivered to those who needed it and much of the aid ended up in the hands of those capable of defrauding the efforts made. It is hoped that the general government, in the case of a world union, would be restricted to the overall planning and equipping of such projects, but that the implementation, delivery and follow up would be delegated to the lowest possible level.

Number 78 begins the discussion of the judicial branch and the powers delegated to it. In this number Hamilton sets forth two of the conditions that were felt indispensable in creating an effective judicial system. First, was the recognition that all federal judges should be nominated by the president and confirmed by the Senate. This has been thoroughly treated above and needs no further discussion here. Second, the duration, or term in office, must be of major consideration. It is generally agreed after centuries of experience that the one condition that allows for the effective, consistent, and proper use of the judicial power is the continuance of judges in office for life, or during good behavior. This, of course, is the main safeguard to the ability of judges to be independent of any type of interest that could sway their judgment; both as to their obtaining a position initially, and in their being able to sustain that position. The latter being the justification for an adequate compensation for their services which can never be diminished. The most important power of judges, in particular the justices of the Supreme Court, is that of interpretation. This power allows them to determine whether or not any particular law, whether of the general government, a state government, or any state constitution is within the intended provisions of the general constitution. The decisions made by judges, or justices, must be free of any type of influence by any person or organization. That is to say the judges and justices must be free from any dependence for continuance in office on any person, organization, or other branch of government. This is the accepted basis of the definition of legal justice throughout the world.

In number 79 and 80 Hamilton deals with the last two considerations to be heeded in the construction of an effective judicial system. First is the jurisdiction to be given the judicial system on the federal level. This includes, at least, six different types of jurisdiction. One, jurisdiction must be granted in all cases arising under the laws passed by the general government. Two, jurisdiction must be granted in all cases arising under the several articles of the constitution. Three, jurisdiction must be granted in all cases in which the general government is a party. Four, jurisdiction must be granted in all cases that affect the general peace, whether between the general government and one, or more, of the state governments; or between, the citizens of one, or more, states, and the citizens of one, or more, other states. Five, jurisdiction must be granted in all cases arising on the high seas, outer space, or other areas of common usage. Six, jurisdiction must be granted in any case where a state judicial system cannot be expected to be impartial. Putting these jurisdictional requirements into words the constitution reads as follows.

"all cases in law and equity arising under the constitution, the laws of the United States, all treaties made, or which shall be made, under their authority; to all cases affecting ambassadors, other public ministers, and consuls; to all cases of admiralty and maritime jurisdiction; to controversies to which the federal government shall be a party, to controversies between two or more states; between a state and the citizens of another state; between the citizens of different states; between the citizens of the same state claiming lands or grants of different states; and between a state or the citizens thereof and foreign states, citizens and subjects."[1]

> The jurisdiction granted in the proposed constitution, which is the same as that of the US Constitution, will not be likely to draw many, if any, objections. However, the second requirement that the laws of the general government, especially the constitution itself, shall be the supreme law of the union will cause some objections to be raised. In some nations, such as those ruled by Islam the objection will be that such laws cannot be expected to take precedence over religious tenets. In others the contention will be that the constitutions of the national governments should be held co-equal with that of the general constitution, and that any controversy should be decided on a case by case basis. There seems to be little doubt that the laws passed by the general government with the intention of benefiting the public as a whole will at times be contrary to particular religious beliefs or other cultural norms. In many cases the controversy would be impossible to resolve in the wording of a general document such as the constitution is intended to be. Instead the controversies that arise will, indeed, need to be reviewed on a case by case basis. This is, in fact, the manner of procedure in the US in relation to all secular laws passed that come into conflict with cultural or legal edicts. It can only be hoped that when the controversy involves a conflict between a secular law and a religious or cultural norm that a solution can be reached which will allow the flexibility to allow exceptions when they are deemed necessary.

In number 81 the power to create inferior courts is discussed. While this issue may have been debatable in 1790 it goes without saying that no solitary court could be expected to handle the daily business of a court system of even a single nation let alone a world union. All of the lower courts would under the existing circumstances need the same jurisdiction that has been given to the Supreme

---

1 *The Federalist Papers*, No.80, p. 236, Great Books of the Western World, Encyclopedia Britannica.

Court. The Supreme Court, on the other hand, would have the distinction of being the final court of appeal. In the US the Supreme Court consists of nine justices, one of whom is designated the chief justice, and is located in the national capitol. Lower appellate federal courts are placed throughout the country with the intention of making them as conveniently accessible to those likely to use them as possible. There are also a great number of US federal district courts that are authorized to stand as the initial court of record. They also are located throughout the country with an eye to the convenience of the public at large. In the US it has been customary to staff the regional appellate, and local district courts, with judges from the locality in which they serve. This system has been shown to be a fertile proving ground for the production of qualified candidates to the higher levels of the court. In our case a similar system is expected to be created and operated in much the same manner. The member nations would of course have their own courts, structured in whatever manner they saw fit, to handle the judicial duties internal to the several nations.

In number 82 Hamilton approaches the relationship between the federal courts and those of the several states. One of the issues handled is whether the state courts would have jurisdiction over matters where the controversies involve a concurrent power with the general government. Neither the US Constitution, nor the one proposed here, speaks directly to that issue. The practice has been established in the US that the jurisdiction of the states and the federal government are concurrent unless explicitly provided otherwise. This allows each case involving concurrent powers to be initially heard in the court most convenient to the parties involved. Each case then would be allowed to appeal through either the state or federal system with the final review being the sole province of the United States Supreme Court. Experience has shown this method of handling concurrent power controversies to be very effective and efficient and it would be suggested that this practice be continued in relation to the concurrent powers contained in the constitution for a world government.

Number 83 handles the lack of specific mention of trial by jury in civil cases. In the US, by amendment, and in our proposed constitution, this right is granted upon request for any case exceeding a minimum dollar amount. It is important that the right of the people to a trial by a jury of their peers be protected in every case in which they find themselves a party.

Number 84 raises the objections to failure to include a bill of rights specifically aimed at the protection of the civil rights of individual citizens. In the US case this was handled by the passage of the first ten amendments to the constitution in 1791. In our case the first ten amendments to the US Constitution have been incorporated into the proposed constitution as separate articles.

Number 85, the last of the Federalist Papers, Hamilton presents an appeal to take advantage of what he sees as the most auspicious opportunity to accomplish the stated goals of individual liberty and justice. The appeal was accepted by a unanimous ratification of the US Constitution in 1791.

In conclusion, it can be submitted that the time is again right for the serious contemplation of an even larger union. The reasons have been set forth as to why such a union is necessary, the reasons why such a union could be successful, a specific method for obtaining the goal of a world union (the constitution proposed herein), the reasons why this method would be the most effective, and the explanations needed to detail how this method would work in relation to the current world political environment. It can only be added that if such a union is not created now it may be many decades before another opportunity as appropriate to the challenge as the one now before us comes around again.

It must also be stated that the US system of government, especially since the end of World War II and the assumption of a world leadership position by the US, has shown itself at times to be very awkward. After the war the US had a specific set of goals in relation to Europe. These goals included the containment of the Soviet Union and Communism, the containment and reintegration of Germany into Western Europe, the creation of a supranational union of Western Europe, and the reduction of the US burden in relation to the defense of Western Europe. All of these goals were consistently pursued during the period from 1945 through the mid 1960's. The unique separation of powers in the US political system made for a rather inconsistent foreign policy during this period resulting in two distinct problems. First the European nations had more control over the programs desired by the US than they would have had if the US system had been more consistent. Second it led to a series of rather important defeats of US policy such as the defeat of the EDC (European Defense Community) by France. It also over the long run led to a less than supranational European Union which also took a much longer time to bring into being than was desired by the US. All of this is pointed out to express the hope that a constitutional convention instituted to bring about a world government will take this glitch in the US political structure into account. This should be of somewhat less importance in a system not based on Nationalism but would, and sometimes does, create logistical problems internally for the US. However, the US system has overall operated quite efficiently in relation to the goals of liberal democracy.

Conclusion

A close look at the problems set forth throughout the preceding chapters should lend themselves to reaching a conclusion. In particular any of the major problems such as the bankruptcy of the existing welfare systems; the collapse of the environment; the abuse of natural resources; etc, can lead to the collapse of the US economy. This collapse, or the collapse of any of the major national economies, can in turn lead to the collapse of the general political system as it known today. The collapse of any of the major economies would probably have a domino effect bringing about worldwide depression or at the very least massive economic adjustments to the new conditions. The failure of welfare systems is not the only cause for economic concern. Economic problems on a worldwide scale could also arise from uncontrolled pollution of the environment; the abusive depletion of the world's natural resources; or the monopolistic control of world markets by a few huge international conglomerates or national consortiums. The same results could arise from the irresponsible use of weapons of mass destruction and the continued unequal distribution of the world's wealth. Future economic problems may also be seen in the current use of outer space and the unregulated use of common areas such as Antarctica and the Arctic. Whether or not regulation is necessary to control honest commercial and social behavior it is needed to control those who would take advantage of criminal or unethical behavior. There can really be no doubt such problems as these can only be solved by planned international action overseen by a worldwide organization. It is the conclusion of this work that this can only be obtained by instituting an effective world government. Currently the only attempts being made to control these and other problems is through the use of international treaties. To date these have been largely unsuccessful.

The arguments were set forth detailing the reasons that the US Constitution should be used as the model or guide for the establishment of a world government is intended to correct this unsuccessful approach to the problems set forth above. In relationship to the realistic implementation of a workable system of human rights, i.e., creating a system that adequately defines and protects human rights under a consistently applied law; and the operation of a general society working within these rights, no better system has been devised than democracy. If the US Constitution is used as a guide, the smaller subdivisions of government, that is, villages, small towns, counties, etc., will be expected to operate under a system of virtual direct democracy. This is to say that in areas of small extent and small populations it will be expected that all of the adult citizens directly participate in the selection, implementation, and operation of the government. In situations that are composed of areas with larger extents and larger populations, such as large towns, cities, states, and nations, it would be expected that the citizens would only participate on a representative basis. In this case they would be responsible for selecting candidates, selection of issues for debate, electing representatives to serve them, and overseeing the performance of their representatives. The actual operation of these governments would be left to the discretion of the representatives elected. The same use of representative democracy would also occur at the level of world government. In this case, however, one further element would be added, i.e., republicanism. In this case the general government would be created by a written constitution that would delegate all of its powers. In addition, the constitution would recognize the equal sovereignty of the nations that made up the membership of the United Nations of Earth. The constitution would also specifically set forth the powers that it wished to deny to the nations, such as the power to declare war and peace. The constitution would also set forth those powers which it specifically wished to be shared concurrently by both the general government and the member nations, for example, the power of taxation. Whatever powers not either delegated to the general government, or denied the members nations, or yet, delegated concurrently to both would be specifically reserved to the member nations or the people. Therefore, the general government would be a Republican Representative Democracy, and the national and local governments would be either Representative Democracies or Direct Democracies. The US Constitution contains a provision that one of the duties of the general government will be to guarantee a representative democratic government to each member and all its local subdivisions. This is, of course, a direct result of the fact that all thirteen states, and their local subdivisions, already had and were operating under some form of democratic government. This will not be true at the institution of a general government for the United Nations of Earth, if in fact, that occurs in the near future. Currently there are several nations that have governments that are either socialist or communist in structure; and in addition there are nations that operate under some form of totalitarian government, such as secular Islam, monarchies, dictatorships, etc. The question is whether or not a constitution used to form a general government for a United Nations of Earth can be constructed to include this type of diversity in governmental forms? If the US Constitution is used as a strict guide the answer would be a definite "no". Assuming that the constitution actually used, however, did take the existing governmental forms into consideration what would be the likely consequences? At the very least, some provision would have to be made to allow for equality within the union for the selection of political candidates, the debate of political issues of a worldwide scale, and the participation of all people in that government. The latter requirement cannot be satisfied in any of the forms of government listed, at least, as they operate today. The assumption that a Republican Representative Democracy would be used in the creation of the United Nations of Earth and that all nations would become members either initially, or shortly after its formation entails at least one additional hope. It would include the desire that all nations would, over a short period of time, adopt some type of democratic government. This may be an impossible requirement. There is, however, no reason outside of procedural problems that would prevent the construction of a general government that allows the greatest level of participation possible; to the greatest number of citizens, under the conditions that exist. It may prove, after several years of operation that such a system is unworkable and that all members will be required to maintain a democratic form of government. As we have seen this appears to be the trend worldwide since World War II and would only require a purposeful acceleration to ratify the new world government.

Our conclusion contains the unstated assumption that the general government has been modeled after the US example and that all nations have become democratic members of the union. It is also assumed, although again unstated, that any nation that voluntarily decided not to join the union would soon find its position outside the union untenable and would seek admission within a short period of time. The conclusion that the world union is possible, practical, and capable of immediate institution on the basis of using the US Constitution as a guide is set forth without equivocation here.

Once an effective world union is established it will be faced with several immediate problems for which there is no historical precedence. In fact, two of these problems will need to be faced either prior to the formation of the union or in connection with its establishment. First, the union cannot be established with any certainty of its success unless the member nations are willing to totally disarm themselves. Total disarmament, in this case, means the total elimination of all weapons, both those of mass destruction and of a conventional nature; the destruction and safe disposal of all existing weapons under a verifiable system of inspection to insure compliance. If there are some nations, at this time, that have voluntarily chosen to remain outside the union the union will need to obtain treaties from them to include them in the general disarmament. The only weapons that would remain in existence would be those needed by the general government to insure the peace of the union; and those needed by the member nations, and their local subdivisions, for the control of criminal behavior. It is assumed, of course, that these weapons would all be conventional in nature and limited to rather small effect. Included within the general disarmament plan must be a method or policy to cope with the high level of economic readjustment that would be needed to replace the existing military/industrial complexes and their service industries. A lot of discussion has already been offered in relation to this problem and the conclusion has been reached that there is no valid reason why a general disarmament could not be implemented and be successful. Second, for the union to be created under the conditions set forth herein the proposed member nations would need to establish a convention directed to the task of writing the actual constitution. Within this task would be the separate tasks of determining the limits of the convention; the method in which the convention was to operate; and the manner in which the constitutional draft would be ratified and put into operation. Again much time has been devoted to the discussion of this problem. The solutions have ranged from using the current U.N. structure, modified to fit the conditions required, to setting up some type of independent procedure for allowing direct public, or national, participation. If the United Nations structure is used the existing veto power of the permanent members of the Security Council would have to be suspended for this issue. If an independent structure was created some consideration would have to be given to the various existing governmental types and the means of insuring a representative participation of all people. Other modifications might also be needed to the U.N. Charter, but in either case the problems to be faced are truly procedural rather than substantive. The use of the existing U.N. structure has the benefit of eliminating the need for the calling of an extended world summit to negotiate the calling of a constitutional convention; and would eliminate the need to set up a worldwide election procedure. If each nation, or in the case of such unions as the European Union or the Russian Federation, has one delegate to the convention then the number of delegates will be two hundred or less. This number appears likely to be one that would lead to an effective and efficient debate on the issues that would face the convention. The final conclusion, therefore, would be that there is no valid reason why such a convention could not be successfully called, operated, and productive of the goal intended. A proposed constitution has been submitted within the body of this work, which was drafted with a strict adherence to the US Constitution. This could be used by the convention as a guide, or the convention could deviate in any manner deemed necessary, but still use the US Constitution as a guide. Once the proposed constitution has been drafted it would be submitted for ratification. Here again the US model is recommended, that is, that the ratification should be the responsibility of the representatives of each nation elected, or appointed, for that sole purpose and that three-fourths of the existing nations must accept the ratification before the new government can be put in force. It is, of course, hoped, and may, in fact, be necessary that a near unanimity be achieved in the ratification process. At some point it will become relevant to detail the issues raised by US history that have directly impacted the concept of Republican Representative Democracy. The US has had a two hundred year plus experience with the operation of a Republican Representative Democracy. It cannot be claimed that this experience has raised all of the most important issues involved in this type of government; or that the issues that have been raised have been adequately resolved. However, the US represents the longest, and most varied, experience with this type of government in existence. As such this experience may indicate the manner in which such issues may be or may not be adequately defined and resolved.

A number of issues have been identified that will undoubtedly need to be resolved in a fashion different from the solution offered by US experience. They include the slow accumulation of powers, not specifically delegated in the constitution, into the hands of the federal government. This trend has tended to convert the existing US government from a true Republican Representative Democracy to a virtual national democracy. The difference being in the manner in which power is delegated to lower levels of government. In a Republic the sovereign powers are delegated in writing by a constitution; while in a national democracy the powers all reside in the general government with delegation of power to the lower institutions being the sole responsibility of the general government. While the current system in the US is still technically a Republic in operation it tends to be more a national democracy. This process has occurred during the period of US history mainly due to the federal acceptance of regulatory, social, and economic functions originally intended to be handled at the local level. This trend could have been averted had the approach of maintaining a separation of powers and duties been more consciously followed. The second area in which the US experience may not want to be used as a model is the growth of a trend away from the selection of candidates, the selection of the political issues to be debated, and the general oversight of representative behavior by the people at large, or by the member states. This recently has included the public's reluctance to even participate in the election of their representatives. It appears from the discussion of this trend that it is due largely to the development of political parties and national interest groups. A second factor has been the demise in the US of a depth in intermediate social organizations, such as the PTA, the Lions Club, and the Chamber of Commerce, among many others, which tended to promote debate on important local and state issues. The loss of this type of cultural medium existing between the nuclear family and the government is felt to have produced a large share of the apathy displayed by the US public towards politics in general. It is likely that the development of alternative systems, such as political parties and interest groups, for the selection of those who hope to serve as representatives and the issues they will debate, should be avoided if at all possible in relation to a world government. Lastly, the US has had a rather dismal record in relation to the arena of civil rights. It has on occasion been ruled by the emotional wasteland of racial and ethnic hatred and discrimination. Every citizen has not been accorded an equal opportunity for personal development either by the social structure or before the law. Although the US has consistently proclaimed its adherence to the underlying ideological principles of the equality of men, and the right to pursue life, liberty, and happiness it has not followed through on these principles. Public pressure has been responsible for the elimination of some of the worse abuses of civil rights but much remains to be done. World government to avoid the consequences obtained in the US must clearly recognize the underlying causes of this abuse of civil rights, that is to say, the failure to eliminate ignorance, poverty, drug dependency, and welfare dependence. The failure to correct these deformities within the social structure has allowed them to tend to become a way of life; one that is generally shunned by the society at large. It should be understood, however, that racial and ethnic hatred and discrimination is a matter of individual choice that the government has very little power to alter. The best that can be achieved by the government is the setting of reasonable standards of treatment that can be expected by all citizens and the institution of a system where abuses of these standards can be eliminated.

It is certain that the establishment of a world government will require a substantial reduction, or sacrifice, of sovereignty in the member nations. It will require that this loss of sovereign powers be accompanied by a national commitment to join in joint decisions, to abide by these joint decisions, and to strive to protect the civil rights of their citizens in relation to the general standards jointly determined. What these standards cannot, and should not attempt, to accomplish is an absolute equality of every citizen before the law. In the US currently the legal equality of citizens has been pushed beyond the natural limits of equality, i.e., the legal system categorically states that all citizens regardless of their physical handicaps, mental disabilities, or emotional condition are equal in reality. This has also been extended to those who through their criminal or immoral behavior have voluntarily given up their right to equal treatment with those who refrain from criminal or immoral behavior. What can be emphasized is that all such persons are equal in the sense of their human status, but, in fact, under certain determined circumstances received different treatment. Every person, however, is, or should be, accorded the right to live a life that is dignified.

In the final analysis the need for a world government, or something related to such a government, has never been greater. The lack of progress on the most important environmental issues, including climate change, is unacceptable. If the warnings that are being issued by the world's scientific community are accurate there would appear to be a rather limited window of opportunity to face these environmental issues. It also is clear that these issues are not going to be resolved through the use of treaties and other arrangements made by two hundred plus nations. If they are to be handled at all, especially in a rapid efficient manner, they will be handled only by a worldwide organization with the power to enforce its commands. This would in all likelihood be a world government.

In the meantime the effects of climate change seem to be producing and will continue to produce much stronger natural storms such as Hurricanes. Global warming also seems to be playing a part in creating greater floods, greater draughts, and other climatic alterations. This has increased the amount of starvation and general poverty over large portions of the earth. Even in the relatively mild area of responding to natural disasters such as Hurricane Katrina the powers of the national state seem to be very limited. In the case of great floods, earthquakes, and famine they are totally incompetent. Even the existing world organizations that respond to such events have in recent years found themselves floundering in their attempts. Once again only a well planned and strategic response to such disasters will be effective and that only seems to be possible on a worldwide scale.

Natural disasters are not the only problems that will require attention on a worldwide basis. Two of the most important are the continued pollution of the environment on a scale unknown in history and the disposal and safe destruction of toxic waste such as that contain in weapons of mass destruction. Neither of these problems is currently being seriously attended to and it doesn't appear that they will be any time soon under the current system of nationalism. Even the two small nations of North Korea and Iran have been able to defy world opinion and continue with the development of nuclear weapons. Once again a comprehensive attempt to solve either of these problems will require a worldwide organization that has the power to issue edicts and regulations needed to reduce or solve these problems and the power to enforce them. It is difficult to imagine a solution to these problems that does not involve the institution of an effective world government.

The recent melting of the Arctic ice cap has also raised the issue of how the natural resources that are being uncovered will be used. Will they be available to whoever (whatever nation) can get to them first? Or will they be reserved for the use of all the citizens of Earth? It would seem rather naïve to believe that they will be reserved for the use of all when the Arctic is surrounded by developed nations, the Russian Federation, Canada, the United States, and Scandinavia. Once again, only a worldwide organization will be capable of developing the laws, regulations, and edicts involved in using common areas for common purposes. This would include not only the Arctic but also Antarctica, the open seas, outer space and possibly cyberspace. These questions are of the utmost importance today with the development of the global market, expanded exploration of outer space, planned attempts at colonization of the moon and Mars and the extraction of resources from both poles.

The experience of the United States can also be noted to express the conviction that problems such as insurrection and disaster control will not be effectively handled on a nation-state basis. The national response to natural disasters in particular has to a large decree been ineffective and ill defined. The concept of a war on terrorism and organized crime has a false ring from the start. Both activities are in fact based upon political rather than just criminal activities. All so-called terrorist organizations are based upon an attempt to replace or overthrow an existing government. The organized international crime is largely economic in character and is to some degree sanctioned by the countries that contain them. Only within the borders of individual nations can the drug-related activities be classified as criminal. However, should the citizens of Earth decided that acts of extra-territorial acts of insurrection and the activities of organized crime be treated as criminal rather than political or economic activities they can only be contained or eradicated by a worldwide effort to eliminate the causes that support them. That is to say political injustice in the case of insurrections must be addressed directly through the judicial system and victims of organized crime in the case of the drug traffic must be ruled either legal or illegal and handled accordingly. It is hard to imagine a rational response to activities on this scale other than through the efforts of a world government supported by all existing nations.

Lastly, the world seems to be faced with a new type of problem, that is, pandemic disease. Whether one looks at the spread of AIDS or the H1N1 virus, whatever their origins, it is clear that a nation-by-nation response will not be effective. It has not been effective in the past and there is no reason to believe that it will be in the future. Only a worldwide organization and effort will be able to rapidly and effectively respond to such diseases.

The United Nations, the European Union, and even the military federations such as NATO that were set up after World War II show that effective action can be taken by a few or even many nations when the stakes are high enough. None of these organizations was intended to act or be anything comparable to a government but they do prove the point that at the very least a world government is feasible. They would also seem to prove the point that the existing nations are intent on maintaining as much of their exclusive sovereign power as possible. The only way around that is by creating the world government as a representative republican government. The US has the longest experience with this form of government and has an existing written constitution that, refined in light of the mistakes and success the US has experienced in the last two hundred and twenty years, could be a guide in the implementation of a world government.

The final conclusion therefore is that the concept of an effective world government is not a utopian dream but a current reality.

BIBLIOGRAPHY

Fukuyama, Francis (1996), *Trust*, New York, Simon & Schuster

Hutchins, Robert Maynard, editor in chief (1952), *Great Books of the Western World*, Vol. 43, *The Federalist*, Chicago, The Encyclopaedia Britannica, Inc.

Lewin, Leonard C. (1967), *Report from Iron Mountain*, New York, The Dial Press

Popper, Karl R. (1966), *The Open Society and Its Enemies*, two volumes, New York, Harper Torchbooks

Ricoeur, Paul (1986), *Lectures on Ideology and Utopia*, New York, Columbia University Press

Zinn, Howard (1999), *A People's History of the United States*, New York, Harpercollins Publishers.